Photographing
THE SELF

Photographing
THE SELF

Methods for
Observing Personal Orientations

Robert C. Ziller

SAGE PUBLICATIONS
The International Professional Publishers
Newbury Park London New Delhi

155.2
Z69p

For information address:

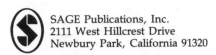

SAGE Publications, Inc.
2111 West Hillcrest Drive
Newbury Park, California 91320

SAGE Publications Ltd.
28 Banner Street
London EC1Y 8QE
England

SAGE Publications India Pvt. Ltd.
M-32 Market
Greater Kailash I
New Delhi 110 048 India

Printed in the United States of America

Library of Congress Cataloging-in-Publication Data

Ziller, Robert C. (Robert Charles), 1924-
    Photographing the self : methods for observing personal orientations / Robert C. Ziller.
        p.   cm.
    Includes bibliographical references and index.
    ISBN 0-8039-3497-1
    1. Self-perception—Research—Audio-visual aids. 2. Observation (Psychology)—Methodology—Audio-visual aids. 3. Photographs—Psychological aspects. 4. Photography in the social sciences.
    I. Title.
    BF697.5.S43Z54   1990
    155.2'028—dc20   90-38949
                                                          CIP

FIRST PRINTING, 1990

Sage Production Editor: Astrid Virding

TP

To
Leslie Lynne Clarke

Contents

Preface

To see the world through the eyes of others is the impell-
ing force for this book. Described here is a search for understanding others by observing at length the views of others
within their environment through photographic images
taken by these same persons in response to a given question. The questions include: "Who are you?" "What does
the good life mean to you?" "What does woman mean?"
"What does war mean?" "What does the United States
mean to you?" Also, "Me and my world?" to a person just
released from prison. The answers are photographs.

"To see" and "to understand" have long been associated.
Indeed one definition of "to see" is "to apprehend as if
by sense of sight" (*The American Heritage Dictionary*, 1971).
Thus it is proposed here that understanding is facilitated
through observation of what the other selectively attends
in the environment. From these orientations deriving from
the interaction of the self and environment, the self theory
of the other may be inferred. Finally, understanding develops as the self theory of the other is perceived.

The book begins with a review of the use of photography
and video-communication as observation approaches in the
social sciences. The advantages and limitations of the approaches are discussed, leading to the proposal of observation from the inside out through auto-photography. It is
also proposed that some of the problems associated with
photo interpretation can be avoided by theory-bracketed
research.

The psychological niche which derives from a theory of
orientations (selective attention in the universe of persons,
objects, and scenes), and the theory of images and meaning are then presented as the guiding frameworks. In
Chapter 2, orientations associated with the meaning of "the
self" are described. Shy persons, for example, are observed
to be less socially oriented. In subsequent chapters, it is proposed that the meaning of critical concepts evolves from an
interaction of the self theory and the environment. Thus,
a more complete delineation of self theory may be inferred
from the study of the personal meaning of critical concepts.
In Chapter 3, for example, orientations associated with such
crucial concepts as "man" and "woman," and "war" are

described. These sections also describe in detail the paraphrasing process in photo-observation, that is, how to move
from images to meaning expressed verbally. The result is
a mixed method of qualitative and quantitative research.

The fourth chapter extends the approach to the cross-
cultural study of values in Poland and the United States.
It is proposed that values influenced by cultural background
constitute a facet of the self which, if ignored, would
misrepresent self theory. Here it is assumed that photography, a form of iconic communication, is a universal
language which may be the preferred representational
system to examine value orientations and self theory
interculturally.

In Chapter 5, the insider's views of the self and world
are compared with the outsider's views. In the comparison
process a basis for explicating cognitive conflict is explored
through insider-outsider orientations toward the meaning
of "the United States," for example.

In the final chapter, the potential of photo-observation
is explored by asking persons who are experiencing critical
events such as divorce and marriage to describe "Me and
my world." Here phenomena are observed by the investigator as they are observed by the actor when and where
they actually occur. Through the camera apparatus, the
doors of the laboratory are opened to the subject's environment, and new facets of the self are observed emanating
from self event interaction.

This small book integrates almost 20 years of exciting exploration. It began when a friend and colleague, Norman
Markel, recommended a graduate student working with
Jerry Eulsman, a photographer in residence at the University of Florida, to work with me on a project relating to my
nonverbal, self-social-schemas approaches to the self-
concept (Ziller, 1973).

In a pilot study, photographic responses were substituted
for verbal responses in the classic "Who am I?" approach
to the study of the self-concept (Bugental & Zelen, 1950).
As soon as several sets of such photographs were available,
I was struck by their "rich revealingness" (see Figure 2.4).
The "self" is depicted within the subject's environment to

reveal the psychological niche. Ever since, it has been an exciting search.

This book also represents the efforts of the friends, students, and colleagues who were companions in this research. These include Brett A. Rorer, Dale E. Smith, Rosemary I. Dinklage, Jeanne M. Combs, Roberto H. Potter, Douglas Lewis, Dolores Corbin, Yutaka Okura and my colleagues, Allan Burns and Hernan Vera.

To John Van Maanen, a separate note of thanks. Your comments, questions, and a key unifying idea were more than a significant contribution to the book. Again, I appreciate the great amount of thought put into your review.

And to Pansy Cheng, who typed all of this, thanks for all your patience and personal interest and for teaching me courtesy through your every gesture. Finally, I am especially grateful to those who shared their images of the world with us. Through auto-photographic observation, universal orientation can develop. Images among persons provides the basis of fellowship across the ages.

CHAPTER
1

Photographic Observation

This is a book about observation of the self. It is proposed that systematic observation is the most fundamental process in the social sciences. It is in this process that ideas originate and are validated. It is the sine qua non of social science. Yet, the topic is usually omitted in treatises on social science methodology, particularly in psychology.

In a classic piece of scholarship, Karl Weick (1985) returns observation to its rightful place in social science methodology. He defines systematic observation as "sustained, explicit, methodical, observing and paraphrasing of social situations in relation to their naturally occurring contexts" (p. 568).

The process is sustained in order to understand the setting more deeply. The emphasis on natural settings must also be underscored. The final and perhaps the most difficult facet of observation is paraphrasing; that is, restating, embedding, or translating an observation so that a more limited and explicit set of meanings becomes attached to it (Weick, 1985).

The objective of observation in the social sciences is to understand the human condition more fully. Understanding contrasts with knowing (see Peltz, 1974). To know requires examination from a position which avoids bias in judgment by bracketing information in some fixed configuration. Knowing is a striving for certainty and categorization where the categorization process is totally controlled by the observer. To understand is to learn more up close from the perspective of the actor, not the observer (see Weick, p. 572). It is proposed here that interpersonal understanding develops when one person considers the other and everything in the environment of the other from the other's point of view. Thus, knowing is egocentric, whereas understanding is allocentric.

Visual social science in the form of still and motion pictures is an obvious way to record what has been observed. Moreover, the critical requirements of observation such as a natural setting, in close, and from the actor's view are readily met, particularly if the photographs are taken by the actor.

Yet since the invention of the camera 150 years ago there has been a paucity of research in the social sciences employing this magical hi-tech observation technique. Recently, however, Wagner (1979) described the use of still photography in social science, including photographs as interview stimuli, systematic recording, content analysis of naive photographers' native image-making, and narrative visual theory. Collier (1975) and Collier and Collier (1986) described photography as a research method in visual anthropology, which included Worth and Adair's classic study of filmmaking by Navajo Indians, where they were found to emphasize walking (1972). In 1972 Ruesch and Kees illustrated nonverbal communication through still photographs, which showed, for example, how body position indicates speed of movement, the status of individuals in groups, and atmospheres in different rooms.

In 1976 Heider described the use of film in ethnography as a way of making a detailed description and analysis of human behavior on a long-term observational study on the spot. Gardner's 1963 classic film, *Dead Birds*, is described in detail. The film was shot over a period of five months and shows battles and funerals as they happened. The use of film in the study of social interaction was reviewed by Kendon (1979) and is exemplified by Ekman's work in the kinesic symptoms of deceitfulness. In 1981, Becker explored the use of photography in sociology, suggesting that the research be related to a theory and outlining problems in the approach such as the validity of the photographs, reactivity in data-gathering, and getting access. Finally, in 1983 Kraus and Fryrear edited a work on photography in mental health illustrating the use of still photography in psychotherapy.

Social science research involving photo-observation can be grouped into five categories: (1) visual records of groups and societies, (2) visual records of human movements, (3) visual records of social interaction, (4) visual records from the actors point of view, and (5) observations involving the interaction of persons and camera. A description of these approaches follows.

Visual Records of Social Groups

Perhaps the origin of the use of photography in the social sciences can be traced to documentary photography. The best known documentary images in the United States were taken by Jacob A. Riis (1890) and Lewis W. Hine (1932). Riis was a reporter who published a series of photographs depicting the abject lifestyles in New York City's slums in the 1890s. Hine, a sociologist, photographed immigrant laborers and working-class children in the factories and mines of early 20th-century America.

It would be remiss not to point out that these documentaries underscore a major problem with photography as an observation technique—the motivation of the photographer. In the early photographs just cited, the photographers were selecting wrongs in an effort to move the viewer to ameliorative action (Campbell, 1983). Moreover, it can be argued that the camera gives validity to any set of appearances whatsoever, contrived as film, and thus is constantly open to the question of quackery (Collier, 1975, p. 136).

Bateson and Mead in Bali

The focus of Bateson and Mead's research was on the relationship between culture and personality and particularly on child rearing. The first book published, *Balinese Character* (1942), used a combination of text and still photographs. The photographs used were culled from a total of 25,000. The authors also shot 22,000 ft. of 16-mm movie film which focused, for the most part, on children interacting with each other and with adults. For example, the Balinese practice of stimulating an infant almost to the point of climax and then suddenly breaking off contact is recorded and is seen as contributing to the "steady state" of adult Balinese. Although it is not entirely clear, it must be concluded that the films were taken to support the authors' major thesis. Nevertheless, theory-guided inquiry can be seen as a requirement of photo-observation. Since so much information can be depicted in film, the process must be guided by a framework in order to focus the observations.

Bateson and Mead also addressed some of the problems associated with the circumstances of photo-observation, such as the question of Balinese camera consciousness, paying for opportunities to photograph dances, and matters of retouching photographs. This was a rare scientific report of the usually unrecorded specifics of the film process required to establish a minimum of scientific credibility.

Visual Records of Physical and Social Movement

The propaedeutic film studies that lead to the film-based studies of social interaction were those involved in the intensive study of human motor development (Ames, 1940; Gesell & Ames, 1937). Michaels (1955) and Kendon (1979) reviewed these studies. The ability to conduct a frame-by-frame analysis of the film derived from a technical development of the camera apparatus.

Film has also been used to study facial expressions (Landis, 1924; Thompson, 1940; Ekman, 1973). Hunt (1936), for example, used film in a detailed study of the startle pattern.

Patterns of body movement in relation to speech have also been studied using photo-observation techniques (Freedman & Hoffman, 1967; Dittman, 1962, 1972). Lomax (1968) made extensive use of film in studies of movement styles in different cultures.

Finally, film has been used to present behavior to observers concerned with judgmental and perceptual processes (Estes, 1938; Dittman, Parloff, & Boomer, 1965). An imaginative study was reported by Nielsen (1964) in which participants in films subsequently watched themselves and gave detailed reports of their own behavior. This latter study is a precursor of the photo-assisted interview.

These photo-observation studies avoid some of the inherent problems associated with trying to record as much as possible about a broad phenomenon by bracketing the phenomenon and the field of inquiry with a fixed camera orientation. In so doing, the nature of the observation is not influenced by the special orientations or attending proclivities of the observer through adjusting the camera field and focus.

Photo-Observation of Social Interaction

The photo-observation approaches reviewed to this point have focused on a single subject at a time, thus avoiding the analysis of the interaction of persons which is a much more complex but common occurrence. Collins and Schaffer (1975) were interested in adult-infant interaction in the first year of life. Moreover, they restricted the problem to having two partners (mother and child) in interaction looking at something other than each other.

This was accomplished by videotaping mothers and infants in a laboratory situation where the room was bare except for four toys fixed to a wall. The baby sat on the mother's knee facing the toys, and fixations of the objects by mother and infant were recorded over a 6-minute period. The data were analyzed to see whether and when the infant looked at the same toy as his mother (and vice versa) with a frequency greater than expected by chance. The mother tended to follow her infant's gaze.

Inside-Out Observations

In the preceding photo-observation approaches, the observer is also usually the photographer. Thus, the photographer's orientations may mediate the behavior and the photo-observation. To correct for this potential bias as well as to provide the actor's view, investigators have asked the actor for feedback about photographs involving the actor. Collier and Collier (1986) describe the work of a creative photographer, Jim Goldberg, who developed an art form of photographic feedback. In his photographic study of the isolation and poverty of homeless people living in run-down residential hotels in San Francisco, Goldberg became concerned about the effects of the circumstances on the spirits of the castaways. To understand the effects, he presented the people with their photographs and recorded their remarks. In the process of photo-interviewing he learned about their lives from their point of view, and he was impressed by their insights, discernment, and the value of their reflections. Thus, through photographs by an observer together with comments about the photographs by the actor, there is a confluence of the insider and outsider views.

A similar but more sophisticated and controlled approach was reported by social psychologists Ickes, Robertson, Tooke, and Teng (1986). The approach described as "naturalistic social cognition" involves a videotape from a concealed position of a 5-minute social interaction between two subjects waiting for the experimenter to find a questionnaire that he had "discovered" was missing. In the second part of the study, the subjects were separated to view identical copies of the videotape. Each time the subject came to a point where he remembered experiencing a particular thought or feeling, the subject was asked to stop the videotape and record his thoughts and feelings. It was found, for example, that social anxiety was clearly related to the number of negative self-thoughts but not to the number of negative feelings. However, a more direct approach to insider observations is accomplished by providing the actors with cameras and asking them to record their own images associated with various feelings.

Just such an approach was initiated by Worth and Adair (1972) who in 1966 asked Navajos to make their own motion pictures. With a minimum of instruction on the use of three-turret Bell and Howell cameras, the Navajos were told to make films of their own choosing and form. This experiment in auto-photography allowed them to act out and produce images of their own conception of the world and their place in it. The results revealed Navajos' cognition patterns, narrative style, and ordering of time and space.

Chalfen (1974) has expanded on the pioneering program of Worth and Adair in a series of studies with lower- and middle-class teenagers. Eight natural groups of 5-to-16-year-olds were invited "to make a movie." Chalfen refers to the final product as a "socio-documentary." Each filmmaking project was recorded by several methods, including a written journal of relevant observations. 35-mm still photographs were taken regularly at different phases of each group's project. Among the observations was the finding that the lower-class groups took more movies of themselves and their friends (doing sports, fighting, drinking), whereas the middle-class children focused on scenes of nature and animals and inanimate objects.

Damico (1985), using still photography in a school setting, attempted to extend these findings to Blacks and Whites. The results were supported. Furthermore, she found that White children included far fewer opposite race photos in their descriptions of the school setting than did Black children.

The actor's view of his/her world through photocommunication was also recognized by psychotherapists in the 1970s. Probably the "break-through" occurred following Akeret's work with the family albums of his clients (1973). Through discussions of these collections of still photographs with the clients, information evolved concerning relationships, personal values, cultures, and ideals. For example, it was observed that in photographs of the entire Kennedy family, including Jack Kennedy as a boy, the females of the family were found in the periphery, the males were centrally located. Other therapists quickly followed this lead (Lewis & Butler, 1974; Wolf, 1976; Combs & Ziller, 1977; McKinney, 1979; Weal, 1980).

Through the insider's view via photography, the researcher becomes a part of the phenomenon, and a personal knowledge is achieved. The researcher begins to "see as they see" and "feel as they feel." Thus the purpose of observation is not simply description and analysis but understanding.

Observing Being Observed

One of the problems associated with observation in general but particularly with photo-observation because of the relative permanence of the image, is the change in the actor's behavior following awareness that he/she is being observed. The act of observation becomes an additional independent variable in itself.

This induced awareness effect has been converted into a virtue by social psychologists in studies of self-focused attention, or the effects of looking inward (Wicklund, 1975; Gibbons & Wicklund, 1987; Carver & Scheirer, 1981). Focusing attention inward in these studies is effected by simply placing a video-camera in the same area or by creating conditions where the subjects see themselves in a mirror. Some of the observed effects of self-focused attention include comparing ourselves to our internal ideals and standards, leading to greater consistency between attitudes and behavior.

In some sense these studies concern observations of persons interacting with the camera or persons operating a camera. Milgram (1977) conducted a series of pilot studies around this theme. For example, he explored what persons tended to be camera-shy, and what distinguished persons who were unwilling to break the line of sight between the photographer and the subject on the streets of New York. Certainly, the miracle-like characteristics of photography are stimuli to creativity. At once, however, this may lead to apparatus-driven research where the photographs are of interest in and of themselves, rather than theory-driven research where the content of the photographs derives from a framework which may include the photographer's personality or culture.

Some Limitations of Photo-Observation

Perhaps the limitations of photo-observation have been overemphasized, thereby retarding the development of the process in the social sciences. For example, early critics referred to photography as "quackery" because of the possible involvement of: (1) the photographer's consciousness, (2) use of equipment, (3) darkroom procedures, (4) editorial processes, (5) juxtaposition of photographs, and (6) context (Gillespie-Waltemade, 1984).

It must be stated at the outset that photography is a discourse between the photographer, the subject of the photograph, and the viewer. The photographer (the observer) is compelled to attend selectively to elements of the potential field of interest. Everything cannot be observed at once, so the observer orients to given subjects for a complex set of reasons, often unknown and unstated. Heisenberg (1958) wrote, "What we observe is not nature itself, but nature exposed to our method of questioning." If then the observer is not aware of the question being asked, the final product may be the result of unknown influences.

Moreover, the target of the communication (the photograph's audience) is an integral part of the communication system and necessarily influences the nature of the photographs. For example, what photographs will be selected to be shown to a given audience or a given experimenter (Blyton, 1987)?

Finally, there is the factor of the subject of the photograph. If the subject is human, the effects of being observed becomes a part of the discourse (see Rosenthal, 1976, for an extensive review of the subject). The basic question is, what effects are ascribable to the process of observation and recording per se? It is obvious that the researcher, in scrutinizing what goes on, is doing something which is unusual and does so for reasons which are not clear to the observed. The effect is exacerbated by the use of a video recorder. Here the record is permanent, and furthermore, captures everything before the camera. The largest amount of noise in communication is introduced when the target of observation behaves for the benefit of the photographer, thereby violating one of the cardinal rules of observation—that observation take place in a natural setting.

By their very nature, observer effects are difficult to assess. How can we ever know what effects observation has, since it is our very presence that is at issue? One solution is to use recording devices operated unpredictably, but even this is only a partial answer.

Weick (1985) has summarized observer effects and notes that observers should not assume that stable behavior means typical behavior; people have strong needs not to examine their lives; one of the most prominent effects of being observed is that people emit more positive behaviors; and the negative effects of the observer as a nonresponsive stranger (an unusual role in an otherwise sociable society) is not corrected by permitting the observers to interact (Barker & Wright, 1955) because that would be reactive.

Weick suggests six ways of addressing the issue of reactivity: (1) examine changes over time for evidence of habituation, (2) vary the conspicuousness of the observer and compare the results, (3) manipulate the subject's awareness of being observed and compare the results, (4) examine if people can be instructed to produce a specific behavior while being observed ("make your child look good"); if they cannot, the question of reactivity is less compelling, (5) ask people about the effects of being observed, (6) monitor behaviors that the target has been made aware with those that have not to ascertain the differential effect of observation.

Explicitness, Orientations, and Self-Observation

The overarching principle of observation which counter-acts the shortcomings and dilemmas of observation techniques is explicitness. "Explicit observation is self conscious, contestable, fully and clearly expressed, and capable of reconstruction" (Weick, 1985, p. 587). Explicitness strives to make tacit understandings of information more evident. The information includes the target of observation, the observer, as well as the nature of the relationship between the observer and the observed, including the lack thereof or efforts to minimize the relationship.

Gouldner has proposed that "honesty is an independent variable in social research" (cited in Douglas, 1976, p. 115). Thus, the observer must be candid about how research is actually done. The observer is influenced by his/her training, inquiry style, current professional and personal activities, and images of people (Weick, 1985).

One of the ways of achieving explicitness is to be occupied with detail. Here is one of the most significant advantages of visual records. But since there is an almost unlimited amount of detail that can be observed, explicitness requires the observer to indicate, at least broadly, the general nature of the observations. In this way the observer acknowledges given orientations rather than permitting the audience to assume that everything was observed and that the specific observations highlighted were those that were the most important ones in some unspecified hierarchy of observations.

It is assumed here that each observer has developed a personal theory of orientations, a theory about what is worth attending to or monitoring. These orientations essentially describe a theory of the self. Thus, if an observer is to be explicit, this self-theory must be made explicit.

Another explicitness-achieving approach is to ask the target to be the observer, but with specific instructions which limit orientations by limiting the range of concerns. Finally, the self-observations can be made explicit through auto-photography, when the target responds to a question by the nonverbal technique of photographic images. Under these circumstance, too, the nature of the relationship between the subject and the scientist must be made explicit. How the photographs are to be used or conjecture by the subject as to how the photographs are to be used by the scientist becomes a variable relating to the results.

Overview

A review of various approaches to the use of photography in the social sciences has been presented along with the limitations, and the role of the observer. In the studies described in this book, the observer is observed. Photographs taken by a naive observer in response to a specific question (i.e., Who are you?) are analyzed in terms of the subject's orientations, meaning, and personal constructs.

Observation by scientists and observation by the subjects are obviously in different domains. For example, "bias" on the part of the scientist must be avoided, minimized, and certainly be made explicit, whereas "bias" by the naive observer is what is studied (presumably in a scientific manner). Indeed, "bias" by the subject is described as orientations or as indicators of the subject's personal constructs emanating from the self-schemata.

Furthermore, in using the naive photographer approach to observation, one additional person has been removed, at least to a degree, from the scene—the scientist. At the very least, this reduces the reactivity or some of the demand characteristics of the approach.

Then too, the naive photographer, in contrast to the scientist, is less aware of the consequences of analysis of photographs, particularly in the unique tasks presented here where there are no precedents. Relatively little theory, social science findings, or scientific expectations obtrude between the naive observer and the photographs. Nevertheless, the scientist as the observer of the naive observer must view the photographs from a theoretical perspective as shown in the following chapters.

CHAPTER
2

Self-Social-Environmental
Orientations
Through Auto-Photography

The self-concept derives from observations of the self by the self. The study of the self-concept is the search for understanding of ourselves and others. But understanding of the self requires a mode of communication about our self-observations that will not obfuscate the response to the query: "Who am I?" It is proposed here that iconic-communication with a camera will produce images of the self that avoid some of the shortcomings of verbal self-reports.

In the process of generating images in response to the question "Who am I?" the respondents are required to selectively attend to a limited number of visual options in their environment. These selectively attended objects are indicators of orientations, and through orientations, the theory of self is revealed. Orientations, then, are the interactive constructs between person and environment, and the most significant component in the cognitive process because of their primacy in the information processing sequence.

In a series of studies, origins of orientations will be traced to the self-concept, where orientations become observations from the inside out. The photo-observation approach to orientations will also be described, along with the method of developing image categories of orientations, approaches to paraphrasing these images, and validating orientations.

The Self-Concept

Although it has only been recently that the self-concept has become one of the central topics of research by social scientists, and particularly social psychologists (see Berkowitz, 1988), the origins of the concept have been traced at least as for back as Homeric times (Reeves, 1958). Here the distinction was made between the physical human body and some nonphysical counterpart described as "social," "spirit," or "psyche." The simplest definition of the self, however, is: "The self is the individual as known to the individual" (Murphy, 1947).

In this definition of the self, the perceptions of the perceiver are raised to a new level of significance. How persons view themselves has significant consequences and is indeed more significant than how the scientist views the person. Persons act on the basis of their perceptions, particularly their perceptions of themselves, the validity of these perceptions notwithstanding. Indeed, this is the major premise and the major contribution of self theory. For example, students' perceptions of their capability in mathematics (self-efficacy: Bandura, 1977) is propaedeutic to performance in mathematical tasks.

The development of the self-concept is not simply internal, however, but evolves in interaction with the environment, including the social environment. For example, how persons view themselves depends in part on how others view them. Others' views are a source of information which may be organized within the personal theory of the self (Cooley, 1909; Stryker, 1980). It is proposed here that everything that is observed by the actor, including the sound of the actor's voice, the actor's behaviors, others' behaviors, scenes, thoughts, and feelings is processed and organized by individuals in an effort to give meaning to their presence and establish a sense of control. Thus, a theory of the self is formulated (see Epstein, 1973).

With this approach to the study of the theory of the self it will be readily noted that different self-concepts necessarily emerge within different environments and in different behavioral contexts. While this may be disconcerting to social scientists in the laboratory tradition, consider this: would it not be surprising to learn that a large percent of modern urban dwellers who had never left their environment, even privately, perceived themselves as hunters? Indeed, the environment and behaviors are the warp and woof of the theory of the self.

Kelly (1955) proposed that everyone, perforce, constructs a theory about themselves. It behooves us to organize in some way, in a personal way, information about ourselves and our world in order to predict and perceive control over our behaviors. The motivations of the actor (self-theorist) are not unlike those of the scientist who seeks to impose order on the universe (Epstein, 1973). The theory of self reduces the task of memorizing a myriad of details about the self through abstraction, thereby achieving a sense of personal control over the universe of information relative to the self.

As is the function of theory in general, new information about the self is more efficiently organized within the framework of the system and provides a system of principles and roles for dealing with the future on the basis of the organization of the past. Once formulated, the theory of the self is a constant active agent in regulating behavioral processes. The self theory of the actor enables the actor to create the environment, in part, by orienting toward certain potential stimuli in selected situations and ignoring others as well as by limiting the repertory of responses consistent with the self theory. The self is proactive as well as reactive (Bandura, 1987; Lyddon, 1988). In this sense, the person develops a psychological niche in which personal control is perceived. It is the region in which environment, self, and behavior are in unity.

The psychological niche is developed through the interaction of the self, environment, and behavior as a system, with the self as a nucleus serving to control or regulate the relation between the environment and behavior. What a person attends to is a function of both the person and environmental features. Furthermore, that which is attended (orientation) is associated with subsequent behavior. By orienting toward a certain feature of the environment (people versus objects versus scenes), that feature serves to limit the range of behaviors possible within that environment. In this manner, shy persons reduce the permutations and combinations of person interaction. Thus, orientations are fundamental to the process of understanding the self. We are what we perceive ourselves to be, which operationalized in the procedure described here is what we orient toward. Figure 2.1 shows the psychological niche.

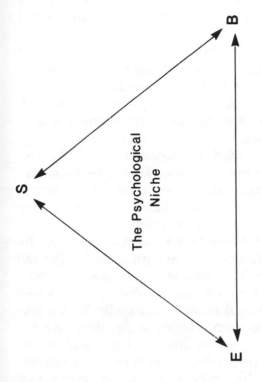

S

B

The Psychological
Niche

E

E = the environment (includes social)

S = the theory of the self

B = behavior

Figure 2.1. The psychological niche: A system of environmental (social)
personal-behavioral controls.

Orientations

The concept of orientations, too, has had a long and illustrious history. In 1927 Pavlov called the orientating response the "What-is-it?" reflex and proclaimed that it lay at the basis of science and culture. Following Sokolov (1963) who renewed interest in the orientating response, Jeffrey (1968) emphasized that the orientating response sharpens attention and focuses it on a certain cue or some salient feature of that cue.

Here, it is assumed that orientation is one of the lowest levels of initial cognitive processes. Pribram (1971) identifies the early stage of orienting as alerting, searching, and sampling. That which is attended at this level provides the bounded field, the information focus of all subsequent stages in the cognitive processes.

But that which is attended is a function of both the person and the environmental features. What something "is" is related to what it means to the perceiver. The perceiver orients to those features of the environment which have meaning for that person (Gibson, 1979).

Here meaning is defined as an interpretation of the stimulus in terms of its significance with regard to the self theory of the perceiver. The self acts as a template or theory of search. In scanning the environment, the search is guided by a self theory which seeks connections with meaningful features of the environment. Orientation, then, are behaviors associated with self-definition which indicate increased motivation to respond to signs in the environment.

Obviously, given the multiplicity of environmental features, there are a multiplicity of orientations. Some of the orientations which have been investigated include self versus task, that is, in a forced-choice situation does the person choose to focus inward upon the self or outward to the task demands (Alper, 1964; Duval & Wicklund, 1972); social or nonsocial—does the person focus on people or on aesthetics, for example, (Zimbardo, 1977); local problems, such as who becomes mayor, versus cosmopolitan concerns, such as transferable skills (Merton, 1949); person loved (Rubin, 1973); cooperation versus competition (Deutch, 1960); past, present, or future (Kahn, 1966); religion (Rorer & Ziller, 1982); self-family-work (Bailyn, 1970); sex (Kupperman, 1967); and interpersonal (Sway & Rubin, 1983).

In order to control for this potential scatter of orientations, early researchers concentrated on laboratory studies where two opposing orientations could be presented in a forced-choice format (see Levelt, 1968). However, the ecological validity of these studies is open to serious question. The range of potential orientations in these laboratory studies has been reduced to the extent that there is little correspondence between the laboratory and field conditions.

The photographic approach to the study of the self-concept via orientations is operationalized in the context in which behavior is evoked, maintained, and modified. In order to incorporate the environment in research designed to enhance understanding, it is necessary to move beyond pencil-and-paper and laboratory approaches to include direct observations and unobtrusive nonreactive measures to the study of lives where they are lived (Mischel, 1977). The present approach uses visual images as metaphors to improve interpersonal communication and understanding. Kelly (1955, p. 268) suggests that if a test "can be arranged to produce a kind of protocol which can be subjected to meaningful analysis, independent of words, we will have made great progress toward better understanding" of the person. It is proposed here that communication through photographic metaphor meets Kelly's criterion, but this is not to suggest that photocommunication is a nostrum or is without its own limitations. It is, however, an additional medium with some unique capabilities for communicating about the self in the environment.

Auto-Photography

As noted in Chapter 1, the photographic approach to orientations has its origin in the seminal studies of Worth and Adair (1972), who asked Navajo Indians to shoot and edit movies about subjects of their own choosing. This approach was described (Worth, 1964, p. 3) as a biodocumentary which was defined as "a film made by a person to show how he feels about himself and his world. It is a way of showing what the objective world that a person sees is really like . . . In addition . . . it often captures feelings and reveals values, attitudes, and concerns that lie beyond the conscious control of the maker." Worth emphasized the nonverbal character of the approach and proposed that the paralinguistics approach makes it easier for persons to talk to us.

In a series of studies by Ziller and colleagues (Combs & Ziller, 1977; Ziller & Smith, 1977; Ziller & Lewis, 1981; Ziller & Rorer, 1985; Ziller & Okura, 1986), the Worth and Adair approach was extended and refocused to study the self-concept by substituting an Instamatic camera for a motion-picture camera. Subjects were provided with the camera, including a built-in flash, 12-exposure film, and instructions that essentially asked, "Who are you?" The following instructions were read or given to the subjects:

> We want you to describe to yourself how you see yourself. To do this we would like you to take (or have someone else take) 12 photographs that tell who you are. These photographs can be of anything just as long as they tell something about who you are. You should not be interested in your skills as a photographer. Keep in mind that the photographs should describe who you are as you see yourself. When you finish you will have a book about yourself that is made up of only 12 photographs.

The subjects were asked to complete the task in six days. Among the first to use the "Who are you?" approach were Bugental and Zelen (1950). They merely provided respondents with a blank piece of paper and asked them to give three answers to the question, "Who are you?" These answers were then classified by mention of name, status characteristic, affective quality, and the like. It was observed, for example, that social references were more frequent for adolescents than for younger children.

Several advantages inhere in the approach. Respondents are able to represent themselves in any framework they please; the approach is simple; and there is a quality of rich revealingness about the self-representation. Some of the same qualities are preserved by substituting photographs (by a nonsophisticated photographer) for words in response to "Who are you?," and at the same time some of the shortcomings of the verbal approach are avoided. In addition, the photographic approach requires gross information reduction, is phenomenological, and may be the preferred representational system for subjects with communication difficulties or across cultures. It would be remiss not to note that members vary with regard to cultural conditioning of picture taking, but these effects do not appear so profound as to vitiate cross-cultural studies.

The photographic self-concept provides only the starting point for the more basic concern: orientation to the environment. By focusing on the self-concept, an affective and motivational component is introduced that personalizes the task, leading to more meaningful content. The study of orientations becomes the study of perceptions outside the laboratory, involving content meaningful to the subject and selected by the subject from a wide range of alternatives. In the vernacular, the study of orientations through photography examines what the person considers worth looking for and looking at. An action component is introduced by requiring the subject to find the appropriate environment, to focus on the section of it that serves as the basis of the nonverbal message, and to make a decision by opening the camera shutter. In terms of experimental design, these characteristics of the required behaviors are less restrictive than are most experimental procedures and thus increase the probability of an association between personality and behavior (see Monson, Hesley, & Chernick, 1982).

It would be a grievous omission not to stress another advantage of auto-photography: subject involvement. In contrast to paper-and-pencil instruments to which the subjects often respond indifferently or even with disdain, auto-photography capitalizes on the inherent interest in photographic communication. Not infrequently, the subjects request copies of the sets of photos, or request to keep the camera for an additional day or more in order to take a particularly "important" photograph. Subject cooperation is high, and there is a general atmosphere of sincerity, perhaps because a photograph is not perceived as a throw-away response, but as a response made in full view of the self which has the permanence of sculpture.

The Explicit Relationship
Between Subject and Scientist

The relationship between the social scientist and the subject was overlooked for too long by social psychologists in laboratory conditions (Ring, 1967). The observer, the observed, and their interaction are components in the social system and will function as an unknown effect in observation unless made explicit.

The auto-photographic approach to observation is reflexive. There is an inherent partnership between the scientist and the subject. By giving the camera to the subject, the subject is given control, just as the scientist-observer communicates control when he/she is in possession of the camera. Thus, the camera is a symbol of control, and giving the camera to the subject is a symbolic gesture of shared control.

The subject's responses—photographs—also create a positively weighted relationship between scientist and subject. Photographs tend to generate positive associations. This response derives in part from the "miracle"-like quality of photographs. Through photography we instantly become artists. Moreover, we are able to communicate vast amounts of information effortlessly. Similarly, the viewer of the photograph is presented with a response which tends to have positive associations. There is a positive response set inherent in the photographic process. As Susan Sontag points out in her essay ''On Photography'' (1977), no one, with the exception of some journal photographers, would say ''Oh, that's ugly, I must have a picture of it.''

This contrasts with the communications between the scientist and subject involving the Rorschach inkblot test, for example. Here, control resides with the scientist. The cards have predominantly negative associations. Moreover, the purpose of the Rorschach is revelations of the un- conscious. The implicit relationship between scientist and subject under these circumstances is similar to that of physi- cian and patient, and the ''patient'' may be expected to re- spond accordingly.

But the inherent positive orientation of photo-observation is readily vitiated by viewing the subject with a jaundiced eye. Even though the camera mediates between the scien- tist and subject, the orientations of the scientist will be com- municated. At the very least the observers' view should be explicit. With regard to myself as an observer, I believe that the subject is to be honored, and that it is a privilege to share the views of others who co-inhabit the earth.

Still this positive ''snapshot view'' of reality must be acknowledged in the interpretation of photographs with regard to the self-concept, as well as the cultural condition- ing of picture-taking already cited. A discussion of these and other related concerns follows.

Content Analysis

The content analysis of the sets of photographs follows and extends the procedures used in earlier research with the ''Who are you?'' approach (Kuhn & McPartland, 1954) and the classic approaches to dream analysis (Hall & Van DeCastle, 1966; Winget & Kramer, 1979).

Consistent with the theory of orientations, the content analysis involves environmental, social, and self-constructs. One example of an environment construct is aesthetic orientation: the percentage of photographs focusing upon the sky, water, flowers, works of art, and the like. An example of a social construct is hedonic tone: the percentage of the total number of photographs involving people where at least one person is seen to be smiling.

By way of illustrating the potential array of categories that may emerge, the following categories were observed in a study of shy and less shy persons (Ziller & Rorer, 1985): groups—photographs showing three or more persons; male-female dyad—photographs showing the subject together with a single person of the opposite sex or a person of the opposite sex alone; self—photographs which include the self; other persons—photographs involving people; touch—photographs showing at least two persons who appear to be touching each other; hedonic tone—photographs where people are included in which at least one person is seen smiling; activity—photographs showing a person doing something, such as mowing a lawn or showing a symbol of an activity such as wood-working tools; sports—photographs showing sports activity or a piece of sports equipment; school—photographs showing books, school buildings, or study activity in central focus; animals—(self-explanatory); religion—photographs showing churches, bibles, or religious symbols; inside—photographs taken indoors as opposed to outdoors; food—(self-explanatory); drugs—photographs showing alcohol or any other type of drug; cars—(self-explanatory); stereo—(self-explanatory); television—(self-explanatory); aesthetic—photographs showing works of art, trees, lakes, ponds, or flowers; range of orientation—the number of categories used to code a set of photographs for one subject (see Figure 2.2).

In this study of shyness, two raters independently coded each set of photographs according to the 20 categories. Interrater reliability for categories ranged from .83 to 1.00. The validity of the categories is suggested in previous research where self, activity, and school orientations were manifested less by psychotherapy clients than by controls (Combs & Ziller, 1977); aesthetic orientations were manifested less by delinquent adolescents than by a control group, and less by persons scoring low as opposed to high on the Allport-Vernon-Lindsey indicator of values (Ziller & Smith, 1977); college students with high as opposed to low grade-point averages showed more books in their photographic self-concept (Ziller & Rorer, 1985); and persons with low self-esteem showed fewer photos including themselves (Cairnes, 1980). Since photographs are "infinitely describable," a multiplicity of coding categories may be expected, rendering validation difficult. Thus, the research associated with this approach must be described as exploratory, with some exceptions.

As has already been explained, a multiplicity of orientations are possible as a result of person-situation interaction as well as the nature of the question. Thus, even though earlier research can be relied upon to provide some of the categories which tend to be universal, such as "self," "people," or "religion," all the photographs presented must be examined anew to determine the emergence of any heretofore unrecognized category of photographs.

The first step in the development of coding categories requires the display of the entire field of sets of photographs. These photographs are examined against the list of categories used in the "Who are you?" and dream research previously cited, and those categories which are found useful in organizing the current photographs are included for coding.

Because of the special nature of the group being studied, the environment, and the focus provided by the question, commonalities among sets of photographs are observed and a new category may be named, such as "touch." This new category emerged in a study of the quality of life of married couples where it was observed that two persons

Figure 3.3 Photographic self-portrait of a shy person.

depicted in a single photo are sometimes in sufficiently close proximity that they are in physical contact or have reached out to make physical contact. Previous research using verbal reports would not proffer such opportunities for this emergent category.

In developing categories, it is helpful to return repeatedly to the photographs to search for new groupings. It is also beneficial to ask a wide variety of persons to enter the room where the photographs are displayed and to unhurriedly study the photographs for categories that they perceive are related to the question posed (see Collier & Collier, 1986, p. 181). The most apparent categories are easily overlooked, such as animals, including pets, or aesthetic orientation, which was described earlier as an example of such an emergent category. Similarly, in Worth and Adair's study of the movies taken by American Indians it was observed that the Indians were oriented toward "walking"; that is, a large percent of the film footage showed persons walking.

When a tentative list of categories has been developed with regard to a given project, categories that are too similar may be omitted (it is not assumed that the categories are independent). Then having developed the revised list of categories, it is helpful to code sets of photographs on a trial basis and to continue to search for new categories or remove redundant categories.

The difficulty of photo-analysis devolves, in part, from the nature of the medium of communication: photography. A single photograph contains megabits of information in a configuration represented in a single image. Each photograph may be coded by one or more categories. Thus, the categories derived from the analysis of words, even when the words describe dreams, will not transfer directly to the analysis of images. The coding of an image, a configuration of bits of information, requires prolonged contemplation (Becker, 1981). In photo-observation, however, prolonged contemplation is made possible by the magnification of time or slow-motion observation because the image is frozen.

Yet another approach to the development of categories is again easily overlooked: consulting the person who took the photographs, the subject. In several of the studies which will be described here, photograph-assisted interviews were conducted. In the study of counselees (Combs & Ziller, 1977), the photographic self-concepts were used in one or more therapy sessions to facilitate communication between the client and therapist. In the course of the interchange, the meaning of the photographs emerged, and categories for the photographs evolved when compared with the control group.

The final and seemingly ultimate approach to the development of categories for the photographs is semiotics, the study of signs (Barthes, 1985; Sebeok, 1978). Barthes refers to the photograph as a "message without a code." He proposes that the meaning of the photographs comes from the objects photographed, which are elements of signification or the interpretation of a sign. The objects are "signs" in that they stand for something or somebody. In the approach to the meaning of photographs presented here, the objects are the signs. Since there is usually more than one object displayed in each photograph, each photograph may be expected to be coded in several ways and may even require coding objects which are excluded in a set of photographs.

For example, a set of photographs are shown in Figure 2.2 which were taken by a shy person in response to the question "Who are you?" Perhaps, most significantly, no persons are focused upon in these photographs. On the other hand, several of the photographs are easily coded as aesthetically oriented.

So the content analysis is guided by previous research with the "Who are you?" approach, dream analysis, the reduction in alternatives because the photographs are taken in response to a specific question, discussions of the photographs with the subjects, and semiotics. Nevertheless, since the photographs are indeed "infinitely describable," the origins of the categories are open to question. Considering the theory of orientations, questions must be raised about the "orientations" of the person who develops the categories. Even with the guides described above, the selective attention of the person developing the categories will be related to the final list of categories. In developing categories for the "shyness" photographs, for example, a psychoanalytically-oriented scientist may very well present a markedly different list of categories. However, when the guidelines for categorization described above are provided to different groups who are given a generous amount of time, I have not found, to date, that the additional groups develop a list of categories that is appreciably different.

The Signification or Meaning of Categories

The meaning of some of the signs or categories, such as "self," "people," "books," "aesthetics," and so forth are described experimentally by moving from the known to the unknown and taking the necessary interpretive step.

Book Orientations

In the first approach, the meaning of book orientation was examined. A series of studies follows which demonstrates the power of the approach. Two groups of subjects with contrasting characteristics (high versus low grade-point average college students) are asked to complete the "Who are you?" task. The focused category is books. Which group shows the object, and which group does not or shows the object less?

It was found (Ziller & Lewis, 1981) that students oriented toward books achieved a higher grade-point average (M_1 = 3.19, M_2 = 2.83, n_1 = 25, n_2 = 56, t = 2.00, $p < .05$). Thus, it is proposed that for college students, orientation toward books is associated with achievement.

Aesthetic Orientation

In an early exploratory study of auto-photography (Ziller & Smith, 1977), a comparison was made between the photographic self-concept of male (n = 20) and female (n = 22) volunteer subjects from two social psychology classes at the University of Florida. Males showed a lower percentage of photographs with plants (5% versus 27%). Assuming an association between female—aesthetics—plants, it was tentatively proposed that the inclusion of plants in the photographic self-concept is an indicator or sign of aesthetic orientation.

In order to escape the controversy which attends ontological arguments associated with aesthetics, a behavioral definition was used. An "aesthetic attitude is attending closely to a work of art (or a natural object)" (see Dickie, 1964).

Here attending is translated into "taking a photograph of." But of what? Inspection of photographic self-concept submitted by students in earlier studies led to the following list of images categorized as "aesthetic": potted plants, trees, shrubs and flowers, scenes, and art objects.

To test the validity of the construct, "aesthetic orientation," 42 volunteers from two psychology classes first completed the photographic self-concept task and then the Vernon-Allport-Lindsey Study of Values, which includes an aesthetic value scale. The percentage of photographs by each subject that depicted one or more of the signs of aesthetic orientation was used on the index of aesthetic orientation. Interrater reliability of the ratings of the subjects was .74. The resulting correlation coefficient between the two scores was .34 (n = 42, p < .05). The link between orientations and performance as well as orientations and values supports the underlying framework.

Self-Orientation

In a study involving 92 children who were 10 years of age in Northern Ireland, Cairnes (1980) found that children who took more photographs showing themselves in the "Who am I?" task also showed higher happiness scores on the Piers-Harris questionnaire ($r = .22$, $n = 92$, $p < .05$), and higher self esteem scores on Coopersmith's questionnaire ($r = .28$, $n = 45$ [boys], $p < .05$).

Social Orientation

In the same aforementioned study it was furthermore found that those children who showed more people also scored higher in social interest on the Ziller Social Schemas Tasks ($r = .25$, $n = .92$, $p < .05$; Ziller, 1973).

Hierarchy of Orientations

A second approach to developing a lexicon of orientations is to describe the hierarchy of orientations used by two known contrasting groups of persons. Thus, it was hypothesized that a complex woman in comparison with a less complex woman will present a photograph of herself more often in a sequence of 12 photographs taken in response to the "Who am I?" question. The hypothesis derives from the proposal that more complex women are less likely to show a photograph of themselves in the self-portrayal series because they do not wish to be categorized on the basis of appearance. Previously, complex persons were found to prolong information search, and it is assumed that prolonged information search about the self can be effected by avoiding premature closure under circumstances of interpersonal perception. Complexity of the self-concept (Ziller, Martel, & Morrison, 1977) is a measure of differentiation derived from an adjective checklist, where the more adjectives checked as relative to the self is associated with higher self-complexity.

The results of the experiment supported the hypothesis at the .05 level of confidence. The mean number of self-photographs for the low complexity women was 7.55 ($n = 11$), whereas the mean number of the self-photographs for high self-complexity women was 4.27 ($n = 11$, $t = 2.05$).

Thus, self presentation in the photographic self-concept sequence of photographs for women is an indication of low
complexity of the self-concept. A more extensive use of the
hierarchical approach to category validation is demonstrated
in the following study of person-environment interaction.

Study 1: Shyness-Environment Interaction[1]

The protracted controversy concerning personality traits
or states has assumed a dialectic position involving person-
situation transaction (see Furnham & Argyle, 1981). It is proposed that we continuously influence the situations of our
lives as well as being affected by them in mutual, molar interactions (Mischel, 1977). These interactions reflect not only
our relations to conditions but also our active selection and
modifications of conditions through our own choices, cogni-
tions, and actions (Wachtel, 1973; Snyder, 1981). For example, once an environment has been selected, that environment in turn serves to limit the range of behaviors possible
within that environment. The mutual interaction between
person and conditions becomes evident when behavior is
studied in the interpersonal contexts in which it is evoked,
maintained, and modified.

A photographic approach to the study of person-
environment interaction is proposed here. The personality
characteristic examined is shyness. Differences in the
selected environments of shy and less shy persons provide
a context for understanding how the selected environments
redound to the shy person to influence the conditions of
shyness. Thus, it is proposed that shyness both induces and
is induced by the perception of the environment.

The Study of Shyness

According to dictionary usage, the term *shy* refers to being uncomfortable in the presence of and avoiding contact

with other people. The research by Zimbardo (1977) follows this definition and equates shyness with a type of people phobia: "to be shy is to be afraid of people, especially people who for some reason are emotionally threatening" (p. 12). Later Leary and Schlenker (1981) defined shyness as a state of social anxiety resulting from contingent interactions in which no event has threatened the individual's social image.

Zimbardo notes five general perspectives on the causes of shyness: (a) personality-trait analyses that focus on innate dispositions, (b) behavioristic analyses that focus on the learning of inappropriate or incorrect social skills, (c) psychoanalytic analyses that view shyness as a symptom of underlying unconscious impulses, (d) sociological analyses that focus on "social programming" and the institutionalization of isolation, and (e) attributional analyses of shyness as a labeling process. It is noted that the first three are essentially person-centered, whereas the last two may be broadly classified as situation-centered. By far the most work on shyness has focused on the identification of it as a personality trait (see Crozier, 1979, for a review of these studies). Cattell (1973), for example, considers shyness to be one component of the H-negative or threctic personality.

Indeed, less negative aspects of shyness are rarely if ever noted. This negative orientation toward "shy" persons may derive from differences in actor-observer attributions where the cause of the behavior is perceived by the observer as attributable to relatively stable negative characteristics of the actor. The shy actor, on the other hand, may attribute his/her behavior to the situation. Nowhere, however, is any information provided concerning the actor's view of the situation. In the approach presented here, shy and less shy persons are asked to respond to the question "Who are you?" by taking (or having someone else take) a set of photographs. The results of the content analyses of the photographs provide information about the contrasting psychological niches of the shy and the less shy person.

Study A: Shyness and Social Orientations

An exploratory study was conducted to examine the utility of the auto-photographic approach with regard to the study of shyness. Consistent with Zimbardo's definition of shyness (1977) it was hypothesized that persons who were more shy would indicate lower social orientations as measured by the number of photographs in response to the "Who am I?" question which included at least one person. In addition, the Eysenck Introversion-Extraversion Scale was administered as well as the Stanford Shyness Survey (Zimbardo, 1977) to triangulate the validity of the approach to orientations. In earlier research (Diener, Larsen, & Emmons, 1984) extraversion was found to correlate with time spent recreating socially ($r = .32$, $p < .01$).

Subjects and Procedure

The subjects were 14 male and 15 female volunteers from an introductory social psychology class at the University of Florida. All the volunteers were included in the study. No credits or rewards accompanied participation.

Instruments

The instructions for the photographic task were the same as those already presented. A Keystone Instamatic 110-mm camera with a built-in flash attachment loaded with a 12-exposure cartridge of film was used.

The loaded cameras were given to the subjects on a Thursday and were to be returned by the following Tuesday. Additional time was provided if requested. The measure of shyness was derived from Zimbardo's (1977) self-report shyness instrument.

Coding

The photographs were coded independently by two persons as to the number of photographs in a set which included at least one person. The few differences in coding were discussed to agreement.

Results

The relationship between shyness and percentage of photographs depicting people was $r(27) = -.50, p < .007$ (shyness is related to fewer photographs showing people), and between percentage of photographs depicting people and the I-E scale was $r(27) = .33, p < .08$ (introversion is related to fewer photographs showing people). Finally, shyness and extraversion were inversely correlated, $r(27) = -.40, p < .03$.

In order to compare Zimbardo's shyness index with the I-E Scale as indicators of social orientation as shown in the photographic self-concept, partial correlations were calculated between shyness and percentage of photographs depicting people (partialing I-E scores) and between the I-E Scale and percent of photographs depicting people (partialing shyness scores). The results were $r(27) = -.39, p < .05$ for shyness and $r(27) = .27$, n.s. for introversion. These results support the validity of the shyness index and also indicate that the shyness index and I-E scale are not interchangeable.

Conclusion

The results of the preliminary study indicate a moderately high association among the three variables and support the hypothesis associating shyness with exclusion of people in the photographic self-concept. Indeed, given the nature of the correlation, it may be advantageous to use the depiction of people in the photographic self-concept as a behavioral index of "shyness" or, preferably, "social orientation" because of its less negative and more descriptive character. Moreover, "social orientation" correlated with Introversion-Extraversion almost at the same level as time spent recreating socially ($r = .33$ and $.32$, respectively) as found in an earlier study by Diener, Larsen, and Emmons (1984). Finally, the partial correlations indicate that the index of "shyness" accounts for more variance of photographic behavior than the I-E Scale. Therefore the second study which follows focused on the orientations of shy persons.

The major contribution of this study, however, is toward establishing the validity of the photographic self-concept. It is easy to dismiss the use of photo-communication of the self-concept as a tour-de-force, lacking psychological meaning or significance. Even though the theoretical base has been outlined, concrete evidence was lacking. This evidence for the validity of the photo-observation of the self-concept represents that first valuable evidence for the utility of studying the self-concept, orientations, meanings, and personal constructs through photographic images.

Study B: Self, Social, and Environmental Orientations Associated with Shyness

The second study extends the analysis of the orientations or the psychological niche of shy persons by enlarging the number of subjects and focusing primarily on the environments selected by the subjects as shown in their photographic self-concepts. In terms of person-environment interaction, it is proposed that the selected environment affects the person. In particular, it is proposed that shy persons construct and create a reduced range of orientations which, in turn, provides a more limited context of person-situation interaction.

Subjects

The first 99 students from an introductory psychology course at the University of Florida who volunteered for the study were included and received partial credit for the course requirement of five hours of participation in laboratory studies; 52 of the subjects were female and 47 were male.

Procedure

The procedure was the same as that previously described, although the I-E Scale was omitted. The instructions were also the same, with the exception that the subjects were asked to take (or have someone else take) six rather than 12 photographs. By simplifying the task it was assumed that the subject would be less inclined to be cavalier about the task requirements; even though all the evidence suggests that the task was approached with remarkable sincerity. When the photographs were returned, a photograph was taken of the subjects in order to help identify them in the content analysis.

Content Analysis

The content analysis follows the procedures described earlier, as do the 21 resulting, but not exhaustive or necessarily independent, categories.

Results

Shyness was found to be significantly associated with behaviors related to taking photographs concerning the self-concept. Shy persons showed fewer groups ($r (99) = -.18$, $p < .06$); fewer male-female dyads ($r (99) = -.19, p < .06$); fewer other people ($r (99) = -.21, p < .04$); more aesthetic orientation ($r (99) = +.26, p < .01$); fewer animals ($r (99) = -.24, p < .01$); more stereos ($r (99) = .26, p < .01$); and less orientation range ($r (99) = -.24, p < .01$). No significant gender effects were obtained. The greatest difference in correlations between males and females was found with regard to shyness and people orientation ($r (47) = -.06$, $p < .67$ for males, and $r (52) = -.26, p < .06$ for females).

Table 2.1 displays the ordering of predictor variables from the stepwise multiple regressions. Using Zimbardo's index of shyness as the criterion, the stepping was terminated when no other variables met the 0.15 significance level for entry into the model. Person orientation with a negative Beta value accounted for the largest amount of variance, followed by aesthetic orientation with a positive Beta value, and hedonic tone with a positive beta value.

In a probe for additional clues in the data, a supplementary analysis was conducted using percentage of photos

TABLE 2.1: Stepwise Multiple Regression Analysis of Orientations in Relation to Shyness

Variable	R	Increase in R	b	F
People	.46	—	−1.14	25.07***
Aesthetics	.49	.026	.38	4.06**
Hedonic	.51	.022	.68	2.80*

*p < .09; **p < .04; ***p < .001

depicting people as the criterion rather than shyness. Since shyness is often defined in terms of "people phobia," the percentage of photos showing people in the auto-photographic task provides an operational definition of the concept. Table 2.2 displays the ordering of the predictor variables from the stepwise multiple regression. The stepping was terminated when no other variable met the 0.15 significance level for entry into the model. The variables include male-female dyad, range, and hedonic tone with positive weightings, and shyness with a negative weighting.

The presentation of a pattern of orientations may be a more appropriate approach to the differentiation of the "shy" and "less shy" subjects. A first approximation of this can be achieved by rank-ordering the orientations in terms of mean percentage of photographs in each category of orientation which was coded with regard to shy and less shy persons. These are shown in Table 2.3. Of particular interest are those in the top four positions in the hierarchy. Omitting the category "inside-outside," which is about the same for both groups, the next three orientations in order for shy persons are aesthetic (.28), people (.14), and self (.09), whereas for less shy persons the comparable hierarchy is people (.45), self (.19), and aesthetic (.17).

Discussion

The findings described above emerge from a phenomenological approach to understanding others. Previously, the scientist as observer described shyness almost exclusively

TABLE 2.2: Stepwise Multiple Regression Analysis of Orientations in Relation to People Inclusion

Variable	R	Increase in R	b	F
Range	0.37	—	1.96	58.08**
Hedonic	0.52	.150	1.36	32.27**
Dyad	0.60	.080	1.16	25.93**
Shy	0.612	.012	−.01	2.93*

*$p < .09$; **$p < .0001$

in negative terms. In the present approach, which examines the orientations of the focal person (here "shy" persons), another view is provided, the inside-out view of the shy person. In the process, the environment of the perceiver is described by the perceiver and perceived by the viewer in the personal context of the perceiver.

From this point of view (the shy side), orientations with potential positive values are observed, including "aesthetics" and music ("stereos"). For "shy" persons, a reduced emphasis on "people orientation" may permit higher probabilities of alternative orientations such as aesthetics and music as a subcategory of aesthetics.

At another level of abstraction, however, it is now proposed that reduced range of orientations observed for shy people provides a less prejudicial basic concept involved in "shyness" and "shyness"-related behaviors. In two of the analyses, it was demonstrated that less shy (or more people-oriented) persons show a broader range of orientations, that is, more categories are required to code their autophotographic displays. It was also suggested that less people-oriented (i.e., shy) persons may focus more on various nonsocial orientations, such as aesthetics and music. In the light of these orientations, shyness may be less prejudicially viewed as the establishment of personal boundaries (privacy) or to establish personal control in order to permit alternative orientations. In the process, however, negative attitudes associated with a less pronounced orientation toward people encourage observers to label one who

TABLE 2.3: Mean Percentage of Orientation as Coded from the Photographic Self-Concepts of Shy and Less Shy Persons

Orientation	Shy	Less Shy
Inside	.53	.57
Aesthetic	.28	.17
People	.14	.45
Self	.09	.19
School	.08	.08
Sports	.07	.09
Stereo	.05	.005
Drugs	.04	.05
Activity	.04	.04
Cars	.04	.04
Hedonic Tone	.02	.05
Television	.02	.01
Food	.02	.02
Groups	.02	.07
Dyad	.02	.05
Other	.01	.10
Religion	.01	.008
Animals	.01	.03
Touch	.01	.01

Note: Since single photographs were coded for more than one category, the total for each column will exceed one. The means were derived from the percentage of each set of 12 photographs coded for each orientation.

seeks privacy with the derogatory, readily available, all-explanatory, omnibus term "shyness."

The auto-photographic approach to the study of shyness is inherently ecologically valid. The subject is viewed within the environment of his/her selections (within the psychological niche). An environment is not prescribed for the subject as is assumed in a laboratory experiment and within the outlines of most theoretical frameworks. In the present approach, the "shy" person's view is presented, and it is a less prejudicial view. In this context, the shy person may be seen as one who selects the environment somewhat differently and with a somewhat different purpose. One such purpose may be to present less permeable self-boundaries or as a personal control. Instead of viewing the shy person in terms of a single orientation (as selected and weighted by an observer), it is proposed here that orientations be considered as a hierarchical group rather than individually. For example, a hierarchy of orientations suggests not only a selection of orientations but also values placed upon these as represented by the ordering of the orientations. Thus, "shy" persons value aesthetic orientations and people more evenly than do less "shy" persons (.28 and .14 versus .45 and .14, see Table 2.3).

But even more significantly, less shy persons place people and self highest in the orientation hierarchy, whereas shy persons place aesthetics first and people second in the orientation hierarchy (see Table 2.3). The difference between shy and less shy persons is one of emphasis in orientations rather than orientations in and of themselves. Moreover, one single difference between the groups such as the lesser orientations toward people does not lead to the interpretations of shy persons as "people phobic."

Once one has selected and placed a value on facets of the environment, that environment, in turn, limits one's behavioral alternatives. The effects are magnified through the accompanying interpretations of being labeled "shy" by the actor (the "shy" person) and the observers (scientists and others). In these terms, "shy" behavior is a function of environmental limitations and labeling by self and/or others as "shy." Thus, the personal selection of the environment and the effects of the selected environment on the individual are extended to include the additional effects introduced by the actor's and observer's labeling of the resulting and evolving person-situation transactions.

The ecological approach to the study of personality described here may be easily extended to other personality variables or to persons in special circumstances, where an understanding of the person may be enhanced if the person is observed in their environment from their viewpoint. The following study explores the utility of the approach with regard to counselees.

Study 2: The Psychological Niche
of Counselees[2]

This study was designed to enhance understanding of counselees by the counselor as well as by the counselee through the photographic depiction of the counselee's psychological niche as represented by a matrix of orientations. Again, understanding is promoted through a view of the counselee from the inside out.

Rogers (1951) viewed the task of counseling as the expansion of self-awareness by enabling the client to experience himself or herself more fully in the present. Rogers emphasized the importance of the counselor's ability to perceive the internal reference of each client. Without this empathic understanding, it is proposed that the client will remain unaware of his present organismic experience.

Jourard (1964) points to the importance of self-disclosure to significant others as a means of experiencing the self. He discussed the ability to self-disclose as a fundamental concept for client and counselor in order to help the client move toward a healthy self-concept. It is proposed that the counseling process is facilitated if the counselor can experience the phenomenal field of the client.

The proposals by Rogers and Jourard are readily assimilated within the framework involving the psychological niche where the perception of the "internal reference of each client" as well as experiencing "the phenomenal field of the client" both readily translate to the depiction of the orientations of the client.

Subjects

University students ($n = 22$) participated as volunteers in the study. There were 11 students (five females and six males) with a mean age of 20 years who were counselees at the university clinic, and 11 students matched for age and sex were members of an introductory social psychology class. The counseling subjects were all the clients of a single counselor during two college terms, excluding those whose stated purpose was vocational counseling and three subjects who declined. Each person was provided with an Instamatic camera and a 12-exposure roll of film.

Procedure

The following instructions were given to each student:

Place yourself in this situation. You are sending a series of 12 photographs one by one through the mail to someone you will meet in two weeks. You want to give a true impression of yourself. I want you to take, or have taken, a series of photographs. I also want to know the order in which you plan to send them, so when they are developed, number them from 1 to 12, marking the first photograph to be sent with a 1. The subject of the photographs can be anything you choose, as long as you think it is communicating something about who you are. I am not interested in your photographic skills. The photographs are only a way of communicating nonverbally who you are.

Each student in the counseling and noncounseling situation discussed their photographs with one of the authors. In the counseling situation the photographic self-concept was introduced in the third or fourth session, and the photographs were used subsequently as a technique for clarification of the self-concept. Figures 2.3 and 2.4 show some of the photos taken by the students.

The photographs taken by the counseled group (see Figure 2.2 for an example) were compared with those taken by the control group (see Figure 2.4 for an example) using 10 categories. These same categories were used in earlier research by the first author following a phenomenological analysis of 90 sets of photographic self-concept of college students (see Ziller & Smith, 1977).

Results

The results of the chi-square and Fisher's exact test (Hays, 1973, p. 738) analyses are presented in Table 2.4. Each group

Figure 2.3. Photographic self-concept of a counselee following divorce.

TABLE 2.4: Client and Nonclient Differences in Photographic Self-Concepts

| | Group | | | Fisher's Exact | |
Category	Client	Control	X^2	Test	P
Family	.36	.00	4.88	—	.05
Self	.54	1.00	—	.018	—
Other person	.90	1.00	1.05	—	ns
Past	.36	.00	—	.045	—
Self and other	.18	.45	1.88	—	ns
Activities	.27	.81	6.60	—	.025
Animals	.27	.36	.20	—	ns
Books	.27	.72	4.56	—	.05
Significant other	.45	.72	1.70	—	ns

was given a percentage score for each category according to the number of photographs in which they had included pictures of themselves; pictures of themselves and others; pictures of others; pictures of family; pictures from the past; pictures of activities (i.e., pictures involving sports, musical instruments, chess, parties, sewing, painting, cooking, biking, and gardening); hedonic tone (percentage of photographs involving people where at least one person is smiling); pictures of books; pictures of significant others (friends, spouse); and pictures of animals. If the subject included one or more photographs involving books, a score of 1 was assigned. If no books were included, a score of 0 was assigned. The photographs were scored independently by two coders. The two scores were consistent 95% of the time. Inconsistencies were reconciled through discussion.

The significance of the differences were tested by chi-square for all categories with the exceptions of the self and past. In the latter cases, the test used was the Fisher's exact test (Hays, 1973, p. 738) because of the low expected frequencies. The counseled group's photographs were significantly different from the noncounseled group's photographs on five of the nine dimensions at the .05 level of confidence. The counseled group presented significantly more pictures of the past and of their families. They presented significantly fewer photographs of themselves,

Figure 2.4. Photographic self-concept of a married woman.

their activities, and their books, and their photographs showed lower hedonic tone.

Discussion

The study explored nine facets of photographic self-presentation. The data illustrate that students under conditions of counseling present different facets of self-image than do other students. Half of the counseled group included photographs of themselves. In contrast, the nonclient group presented photographs of themselves in every instance. In view of research cited earlier (Cairnes, 1980), which showed that inclusion of a photograph of oneself is related to self-esteem, the results simply demonstrate again that under conditions of personal stress, individuals reveal lower self evaluations.

Two other facets of client self-concept that were significantly different from the nonclient group were the choice of family photographs and photographs from the past. In the nonclient group, not one person included any photographs in either of these categories in his or her photographic self-concept. The client group may have been experiencing difficulties in defining themselves in terms other than that of a family self-identity, that is, they may have been experiencing difficulty in making the transition from the family setting. Indeed, finding a sense of self outside the family nexus is one of the most common problems of college students (Laing & Esterson, 1964).

A need to return to the past may characterize the individual in transition. Thus, Mueller (1973) observed that a client who is experiencing conflict may seek a less conflicted mode of experiencing, such as reliving the past, or perhaps more simply, seek a reliable support group from the past.

In contrast to the emphasis on the family and the past by clients, lack of emphasis was observed concerning activities and books. Only 27% of the client group included these categories in their photographic self-concept. The nonclient group included activities and books 81% of the time. Subjects in the nonclient group described their self-images in terms of activities such as swimming, tennis, biking, and studying. The client group presented remarkably few activities of this kind as being associated with the self-image. Because a college environment usually includes a variety of these activities, these data suggest that the client group is alienated. Perhaps, again, these clients are experiencing difficulty in transition from the home to the college environment, or more generally, the client group is under conflict and stress that leads to a more closed and less active participation in their present environment. Some turn to the past for orientations. For the present all have recourse to a counselor. Perhaps it is the future that poses one of the significant difficulties, or time orientations in general. The counselee has experienced a discontinuity among life events (loss of a close friend, for example) that renders the future extraordinarily uncertain. Thus, the task of counseling is to reestablish a relationship between the client's past, present, and future.

In one case, for example, the client seemed to present many of the photographs common to the control group. A closer inspection of the photographs showed no books, no photographs of his wife, and a number of photographs from the past, including a photograph of his mother and grandmother whom he visited weekly. The emerging theme was difficulty with the present social environment and an attempt to emphasize continuity with the past.

Using the photographs as stimulus materials with the client as a partner in the inquiry can lead to increased empathic understanding through the delineation of the psychological niche of the client.

The psychological niche takes into account the person-environment interaction. The auto-photographic approach to the study of the psychological niche compels consideration of the environment in understanding persons and imposes ecological validity.

By definition, however, the psychological niche is interactional. Orientations emerge both from personal schemas and from the characteristics of the environment. Thus the counselee selects the orientations to the past, limited activities, and reduced hedonic tone, but then the selected orientations (the psychological niche) become the special environment of the individual and reflexively limits the behavior of the counselee, thereby creating a spiraling effect in the existing directions of development (a self-fulfilling prophecy). In a sense, the psychological niche becomes a social trap. The niche is created in an effort to achieve a degree of personal control, but the niche also limits adaptability to the environment that the person must enter eventually. The quest for equanimity in the immediate environment retards the transition to the imminent environment.

A large number of questions remain to be answered. How can the photographic self-concept approach be used in a counseling setting? How are the counselor's perception of the client and the client's perception of the counselor altered when the photographic self-concept is employed? What are the characteristics of clients who avoid using the approach? Under what circumstances is communication between the client and the counselor facilitated through the photographic self-concept approach? (See Amerikaner, Schauble, & Ziller, 1980; Kraus & Fryrear, 1983.)

It is clear, however, that the approach has several advantages. Clients are able to represent themselves in any framework they please; the approach is simple; the approach is creative rather than reactive; there is a quality of ''rich revealingness'' about the self-presentation, deriving, in part, from the unintentional information in addition to the intentional information, and at the same time some of the usual shortcomings of verbal responses are avoided. Finally, it must be noted that the orientations toward family emerged as a new significant construct for these persons in their environment. More significantly, through the presentation of a set of associated orientations the person's psychological niche is portrayed. The following study extends the study of the psychological niche to explorations of physically attractive persons.

Study 3: Attractive Persons
and the Magic Mirror[3]

The auto-photographic approach to the study of the self-concept is diametrically opposed to the methods usually employed by social scientists in attempting to understand persons. Usually, the social scientist observes the subject's behavior on some task and then seeks understanding by inferring the subject's view. The researcher is in control. Indeed, this reveals the proclivities of the researcher with regard to the observed. The researcher tends to assume a dominant position vis-á-vis the subject.

In contrast, through auto-photography the observed is in control, and understanding derives from the observed's point of view. Understanding begins with the view through the eyes of the observed. In the study described here, understanding of physically attractive persons is sought through the magic mirror of auto-photography.

Since the early studies of physical attraction by Walster et al. (1966), many of the results are introduced with the phrase, "physically attractive persons are judged to be . . . ." A judgment follows by someone reacting to the physically attractive person, although O'Grady (1982) presented the attractive person's view when it was noted that college students who are high in attractiveness believe they are less likely to become mentally ill in the future. The inside-out view of attractive persons was also presented by McDonald and Eilenfield (1980), who found that physically more attractive persons spent more time gazing at his or her reflection. In the present study, the frozen reflections of the self of attractive and less attractive persons will be explored through auto-photography.

Subjects

The subjects were 39 males and 55 female volunteers from an introductory psychology class at the University of Florida.

Procedure

The instructions concerning the photographic self-concept were the same as those given to subjects in the study of shyness. When the subjects returned their film, they were photographed against a standard background in order to establish their identity photographically. These photographs also were subsequently rated on a five-point scale of attractiveness where only the extreme points were defined as attractive and unattractive. Thirty raters evaluated the photographs. The mean attraction rating was 2.5. The reliability of the ratings was .90. The photographs were coded using the same categories as were reported in the shyness study and with the same reliabilities.

Results

First, the correlations between orientations and attractiveness ratings were calculated. Higher attractiveness was associated with more self-portrayals ($r = .44$, $p < .001$), more social orientation (inclusion of people, $r = .25$, $p < .01$), greater hedonic tone (smiling, $r = .18$, $p < .07$), and greater range of orientations ($r = .32$, $p < .001$), but less religious orientation ($r = -.30$, $p < .001$), less drug orientation ($r = -.25$, $p < .01$), and less sports orientation ($r = -.22$, $p < .05$).

Next an 8-variable regression model of regression analysis was calculated for female subjects. This regression technique is designed to capitalize less on chance. The variable gains entry if $p < .15$. Self and religion were found to have positive Beta weights ($p < .001$), whereas negative Beta weights were found with regard to aesthetics ($p < .02$), sports ($p < .0002$), and drugs ($p < .01$). The mean attractiveness rating for females was 3.4 and $r = .65$.

For men, a 3-variable regression analysis was calculated. The mean attraction rating for men was 1.6, $r = .30$. Self was again positively weighted ($p < .03$), but religion was negatively weighted with regard to attraction ($p < .01$), as was drugs ($p < .03$).

A 5-variable model of regression analysis was calculated for the combined male and female subjects ($r = .35$). Self had a positive weighting ($p < .001$), whereas negative weighting was found for aesthetics ($p < .07$), religion ($p < .04$), sports ($p < .14$), and drugs ($p < .01$).

The results support the findings of McDonald and Eilenfield (1980), indicating that more attractive persons spend more time gazing into a mirror. In the present study, more attractive persons were found to show more self-photos in their photographic self-concepts. The current results emanating from self-theory and orientations suggest something quite different than the earlier study, however. The mirror study suggests that attractive persons gaze into a mirror longer as a self-affirmation ritual or as self-reinforcement. It is implied that there is a basic need that is satisfied by this act of self-gazing.

The current framework and accompanying method of auto-photography takes the view of the perceiver, the subject. These results show that a significant facet of the self-theory of attractive persons is physical appearance. But it is not the only significant self-component. People orientation or social-orientation is also a significant selected attention. Thus, by taking the view of the subject as opposed to the scientist-observer, a less prejudicial theory of physical attraction emerges. Thus, for example, it is noted that more attractive females show a wider range of orientations; that is, a larger number of categories of orientation are used when coding the photographs of attractive females. Thus, it is assumed that attractive females have a broader range of selective attention.

Certainly, the psychological niche of the attractive persons is different than that of less attractive persons. The environment attended is different and those orientations redound to the persons and their behavior to create a unique psychological niche.

We would be remiss not to note the provocative finding that religion was found to have a positive loading for attractive women and a negative loading for attractive men. I will avoid the temptation of speculation. This leads, however, to the essential question of the interpretation of the orientations.

Interpreting Orientations

The theory of orientations underscores that selective attention is an information reduction process which provides the base for other cognitive processes. Pavlov based his enthusiasm for the construct of the "orientating reflex" on a similar assumption and realization, as did subsequent scientists in the area, including those who equated orientations and attitudes. More recently, it was observed (Bargh, 1982) that before social information can be understood or processed, it must be brought from the "outside" to the "inside" by some means or other. That is, the information must be incorporated into our cognitive system or encoded. But before this can occur, another more basic step must become the focus of our attention: we must notice it in some way. Attention, then, is the start of the entire cognitive process.

But if attention is the initial step in information processing, and coding the intermediate step, the final step is inference. But this, the most critical step, is insufficiently addressed (Levy, 1963), although Hastie (1983) has described a variety of biases in social inference which derive from attempts to simplify a complex task. For example, the inference process is strongly influenced by available information.

Thus, in the study of attractive persons using autophotography, it was observed that more attractive persons orient (or attend) to the self more frequently; or less interpretively, they show more photographs including themselves in their photographic self-concepts. But what can be inferred from this behavior?

Perhaps those who show photographs of themselves more frequently in the auto-photographic-self task are more egocentric, or more self-aware, or monitor themselves more, or are people who care about how they appear to others, or how they appear to themselves. What is known is that they attend or orient to themselves more and, necessarily, to something else less. Considering the potential objects that could be attended, this fact in itself is of considerable moment. Thus, it can be inferred, at a low level of abstraction, that orienting to the "self" is more important for some reason than orienting to other objects.

The first potential bias of information processing and inference is to exaggerate the significance of a single piece of information. The simple fact that this information is available does not relate to its significance (Kahneman & Tversky, 1972). Thus, other orientations such as orientations toward people and hedonic tone must be considered simultaneously in the inference process.

It can be inferred from the orientations of attractive persons that they are more positively, socially orientated than less attractive persons. The inference process, here, is not unlike that of explaining the factors in a factor-analytic study. A matrix of information serves as the basis of inference.

At this point, this inference is still a hypothesis. In the study of more attractive persons, the data-based inference was tested by relating ratings of attraction to a scale of shyness (Zimbardo, 1977). The resulting correlation was $-.52$ ($n = 97$, $p < .001$). More attractive persons reported that they were less shy. Thus, the category of "people" derived from the photographic self-concept appears justified because it is based upon an established theory, past successes, and representative interpreters (Krippendorff, 1980, p. 101).

Still, this explanation is inferential. The search for under-standing is, by definition, open (see Peltz, 1974). To end the search risks dogmatism. To remain at the level of listing orientations, while more than descriptive because of the severe information reduction properties of attention, is to risk dogmatism at the other end of the scale because we terminate the search and imply "knowing" through descrip-tion of orientations.

Of course, the risks associated with inference from descriptive information is greatly reduced if the orientations are predicted on the basis of a theoretical framework, as was shown in the study of the number of self-presentations by complex females. Having demonstrated the relationship, however, we are left with abundant other explanations.

Yet again, a single observed difference in orientations bet-ween two groups may be crucial, even if it is surprising. In fact, if an observation is surprising, this provides some assurance that it was not created through experimental manipulations in order to be consistent with the inherent biases and proclivities of the none-too-uninvolved investigator.

Thus, in an auto-photographic study of 24 gifted children in comparison with 24 less gifted students (based on teacher evaluations and Stanford-Binet test scores) in the first to sixth grades in a metropolitan school system, it was found that the gifted group was more oriented toward parents (54% versus 21% X^2 = 5.6%, $p < .02$). It is a low-level in-ference to assume that gifted children and their parents have a different relationship than less gifted children. Still, there are many questions that remain. Do gifted children initiate the relationship? Are gifted children more interesting or "mentally attractive"? Nevertheless, the observation is significant because orientations are significant simply on the basis of information reduction.

Thus the inference process in auto-photography is quite different than those in other observational methods (see Wcick, 1985). In the auto-photographic approach, the information is vastly reduced because of the properties of still-photography, and the approach is more focused because the information is produced in response to a question ("Who are you?"). Most significantly, the inferences are based on orientations which themselves represent the first level of abstraction and, are theory based. Thus, the auto-photographic approach affords a ladder of inference moving from photo-focused information (i.e., "Who are you?" photos taken by attractive persons), to orientations (i.e., "self," "people," "hedonic tone"), to second level inferences ("social orientations").

At the base, however, the inferential process is a search for meaning. Here the meaning of the self is derived associatively. The meaning of the self involves images (and orientations) associated with the self. This becomes the thesis of the following chapter.

Overview

The efficacy of auto-photographic observation and the study of orientations has been described here with the presentation of the theory of the self and orientations, the orientation methodology involving the camera, studies demonstrating the utility of the approach, and an explanation of the interpretation of orientations as distinguished from the interpretation of pictures (see Kennedy, 1974). Auto-photography results in photographs that require interpretation, but the photographs are responses to the question "Who are you?" Thus the interpretive process is "wondrously focused." This process is further aided by the nature of camera operation, which involves a lens with a limited angle of inclusion, thereby serving as a severe information reduction mechanism. Essentially, auto-photography is a method of nonverbal communication which provides a frozen image with a message. The message is in the form of a sign couched in metaphor. These signs communicate about the person's theory of the self where that person lives. The psychological niche of the persons is described from the view of the person. A parallel sociological niche is described from the view of other persons and may be sketched through a similar socio-photographic approach by asking persons who are acquainted with the target person to take a set of "Who is he?" photographs. But it is proposed here that this is an abbreviated version of the interpersonal perception process commonly employed. We understand others through images of their psychological niche composed by our own self-theory, the environment in which the target is interacting, and the target's behavior.

Underlying the auto-photographic approach is an association between image and meaning. Here the topic has been the meaning of the self through images of the self. We now turn to the more general problem of the meaning of constructs other than the self through iconic-communication. The psychological niche theory proposes that the meaning of all constructs derive from and reflect the theory of the self in interaction with the environment. Thus a more complete theory of the self will be represented by exploring the personal meaning of a variety of significant concepts in terms of self-environment interaction.

Notes

1. This is a shortened version of an article by Ziller & Rorer, 1980, in the *Journal of Personality*, *53*, 626-639. Copyright Duke University Press.

2. This is an abbreviated account of an article by Combs & Ziller, 1977, in the *Journal of Counseling Psychology*, *24*, 452-455. Reprinted by permission of the American Psychological Association.

3. This study was conducted by Brett Rorer and Robert C. Ziller.

CHAPTER
3

Images and Meaning of the Self

The study of the photographic self-concept is readily reconceptualized as the study of the meaning of the self through photographic images. As such, the topic is but a special case of the more general area of the measurement of meaning through images. It is proposed that the meaning of a concept is the associated orientations or personal constructs (Kelly, 1955; Neimeyer, 1987) and that a more valid theory of the self may be inferred from a broader range of orientations associated with the personal meaning of critical concepts such as "woman," "man," "war," and "peace." Here the meaning of a concept is assumed to develop out of the self-environment interaction following the presentation of the concept definition task. In this chapter the meaning of the self will be extended and shown to be associated with gender and national environments.

The Meaning of Meaning

The term "meaning" seems almost self-explanatory until the question is raised as to the meaning of "meaning." Indeed, hermeneutics has been the subject of study by philosophers and theologians for centuries, but recently social scientists have introduced operational definitions. The approach used here can be traced from Plato (see Warren, 1916), who is often cited as the originator of the concept of association. The emphasis in Plato's thinking was on the association of words to images and to other images.

It was with Wundt's (1883) association experiments ("charity"-"kindness") that the definition of meaning emerged: an associative connection between stimulus and response (Creelman, 1966, p. 207). The relation between images and meaning was originally stated by William James (1890), who defined the meaning of words as sensory images awakened. It was Koffka (1935) and earlier Freud (1924), however, who utilized images in their investigations of the meaning of crucial concepts. In Koffka's experiment a word was called out, and the subject waited passively for an image to appear. The images were usually illustrative of the meaning of the stimulus word, for example "money" —an image of a coin, but of no special denomination.

In the free-association technique used by Freud in psychoanalysis, the person was instructed to give his/her thoughts complete freedom and to report daydreams, feelings, and images, no matter how incoherent, illogical, or meaningless they seemed. Freud characterized the process as a "search after meaning."

More recently, Deese (1965) proposed that the free-association test provides the most useful approach to the general case of meaning. Deese's instructions read, "Tell me what _____ means." The subjects were limited to a one-word response, but he used about 100 subjects in order to obtain an adequate number and range of responses. In the association dictionary he developed, the word "girl," for example, was associated most frequently with the words "boy" and "woman." "Peace" was most frequently associated with the word "war." It is apparent that the approach, though theory-derived, is severely limited. Indeed, Deese himself noted the verbal nature of the task and hinted at the advantages of image responses.

By introducing images as free associations to verbal stimuli, a metaphoric approach to meaning emerges. Bringing an alternative frame of reference or language system to bear upon a set of observations transforms the focus for understanding. Essentially metaphor depicts one thing in terms of another (Ortony & Reynolds, 1978). Here, the word is depicted by a photograph. A bridge is proposed between the known and the unknown through ostensive reference (Petrie, 1979). The photographic response to the stimulus word is assumed to facilitate understanding by an iterative process from the more familiar metaphorical vehicle, the photograph.

The Meaning of Self

In the preceding chapter, the meaning of the self was elicited through photographic responses to the question "Who are you?" Although this central question evokes a wide spectrum of responses and orientations, it at once limits the range of responses simply by reducing the field of related orientations, and thereby limits the nature of the emergent theory of the self and the validity of the psychological niche.

It is assumed here, consistent with the Environment-Self-Behavior framework, that the person functioning within the theory of the self is an agent who construes his/her world motivated by the need to perceive control. In the construal of both the environment and behavior, a psychological niche is developed. The nucleus of this niche is the theory of the self. From the interaction of the theory of the self with the environment, orientations are generated. These orientations are generated by imposing a personal meaning on the environment. Orientations are essentially personal constructs in that they represent personal construction of events (Kelly, 1955; Neimeyer, 1987).

Again, however, since the self theory is assumed to be the nucleus of the E-S-B system, orientations and personal constructs emanate from the self theory; and the self theory, in turn, may be inferred from the orientations and personal constructs. It is now proposed that a more complete and valid theory of the self may be described through images by exploring the meaning not only of the self but of other crucial concepts as well.

Consistent with the theory of the psychological niche, personal constructs emanating from the meaning of critical concepts derive from the self-concept. Thus, it is proposed that the theory of the self is revealed through images of the personal meaning of crucial concepts. Also consistent with the Environment-Self-Behavior theory describing the psychological niche, the environment which interacts with the self also interacts with meaning. The meaning of concepts influences and is influenced by the environment. The meaning of concepts will differ as environments differ. A series of studies will be presented in which the meaning of "woman," "man," and "war" will be explored and will be shown to adumbrate the self theories of persons of different gender and different cultural histories.

The Meaning of "Woman"

In the first two exploratory studies of meaning, the concepts "woman" and "man" were selected because gender represents one of the earliest self-differentiations and categorizations. Thus, the orientations and personal constructs associated with these concepts will contribute to the development of a more complete theory of the self. Moreover, through visual portrayal of the gender differences in the meaning of these crucial concepts, the basis of the inherent gender conflict may be shown to have its origins in basic differences in self-other concepts.

Subjects

The subjects were 46 volunteers (25 males and 21 females) from two social psychology classes at the University of Florida.

Procedure

Each subject was provided with a 110-mm Keystone Instamatic camera with a built-in flash and loaded with a roll of 12-exposure film. The following written instructions were given to each subject:

> We want you to take three photographs that best describe "woman" from your point of view. These photographs can be of anything, as long as they tell something about what "woman" means. Before you begin, it will be helpful to think about the photographs you

would like to take. Take a few minutes to write your ideas. You can use these suggestions for your photographs. You should not be interested in your skill as a photographer but only in your photographic description of "woman." When completed you will have presented a three-photograph essay on "woman."

Subjects received the cameras on a Thursday and were asked to return them the following Tuesday to allow photographs to be taken over the weekend.

Content Analysis

The analysis of the sets of photographs followed the earlier procedures. However, since the question was different, different coding categories were expected (see Figures 3.1 and 3.2).

The following categories of the photographs emerged after inspection of the entire set by a naive group of observers: indoors versus outdoors (photographs in a set taken indoors as opposed to outdoors); people (photographs in a set including at least one person as focal target); child (photographs in a set including at least one child as focal target); male (photographs in a set showing at least one male); groups (two or more persons as a focal target); activity (photographs in a set representing a person or persons engaged in some motion as opposed to an attitude of inaction); task orientation (photographs in a set representing bicycling, skating, tennis, mountain climbing, fishing, and the like); sensuous (photographs in a set depicting a woman in a bathing suit, underclothes, lying on a bed, and the like); proximity or closeness (photographs in a set showing two or more persons in bodily contact); and orientation range (the number of categories used in coding each set of photographs).

Results

The photographs were coded independently and blindly by a male and female. The reliability of the codings ranged from .60 to 1.00.

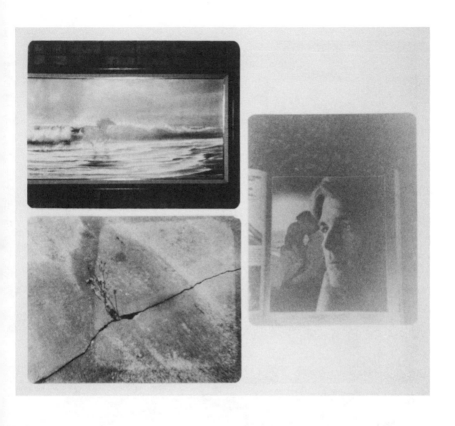

Figure 3.1. The image meaning of ''woman'' by a woman.

Figure 3.2. The image meaning of ''woman'' by a man.

It was found that females in comparison with males showed a higher number of photographs with children (M_1 = .31, M_2 = .03, F = 4.70, p < .003), of groups (M_1 = 1.00, M_2 = .35, F = 8.72, p < .004), of activity (M_1 = 1.00, M_2 = .35, F = 9.33, p < .003), of task orientation (M_1 = .61, M_2 = .27, F = 3.98, p < .05), proximity or closeness (M_1 = .56, M_2 = .16, F = 11.8, p < .001), and orientation range (M_1 = 11.6, M_2 = 9.2, F = 2.04, p < .05). Males more frequently than females showed images with an outdoor orientation, a male, and sensuous denotations, but none of these latter results approached statistical significance.

Discussion

The results demonstrate some of the self-defining personal constructs of women. Women (in contrast to men) view themselves as more socially oriented and more activity oriented. It is assumed that these personal constructs have their origins in the socialization process deriving from gender roles and gender categorization. Women are expected to be more socially involved (Gilligan, 1982; Broverman et al., 1972). In terms of role theory (Biddle & Thomas, 1966), roles defined in terms of expected behavior consistent with position in a social system are congruent with self-definition. The self-concept is related to the role played in society. The roles associated with women are differentiated from those of men, leading to differences in the self-concept which are shown here in terms of personal constructs.

Indeed, the meaning of "woman" for woman is probably formulated, in part, in terms of comparison and contrast with the meaning of man as the concept of man is perceived by women. Since "man" and "woman" represent separate groups of persons in most societies, the comparison process involves the in-group/out-group phenomena (Tajfel, 1970, 1978; Allen & Wilder 1975; Turner, 1981).

These aforementioned studies describe the surprising consequences of simply dividing a collection of persons into two subgroups on the basis of some trivial distinction, such as overestimating or underestimating on a dot-estimation task. When faced with a choice between allocating rewards to an in-group member or an out-group member, they favored the in-group at the expense of the out-group.

The results of the study described here suggest even more profound consequences of the development of antipodal categories of persons, namely, the creation of different environments for the two groups and the reduced opportunity for members of the separate groups to observe the other group members in their own environment. This results in the development of special conceptual systems which can lead to psychological separation of the groups and the increased potential for conflict deriving from cognitive differences.

The results of the current study suggest that male's perception of woman is more stereotypic; that is, it shows a more limited use of categories or associations for the meaning of woman. As an out-group member, the male as observer may be inclined to scan the environment of the female for contrasts to the environment of males, and to simplify the task by reducing the field to the stereotypic category "female" in describing the out-group members. Indeed, in-group/out-group research (Rothbart, Dawes, & Park, 1984; Wilder, 1984) has supported the "out-group homogeneity" hypothesis ("they all look the same to me"). Simply stated, it is proposed that people perceive more variability in the characteristics of their own group than in the characteristics of out-groups.

Images of "Man"

The preceding study of images of women was followed by a companion study of images of man in order to compare gender views.

Subjects

The subjects were composed of two groups: a working group consisting of 12 males and 12 females ranging in age from 40 to 48 and a student group consisting of 12 males and 12 females ranging in age from 17 to 22. Again the subjects were all volunteers and received no rewards for participating in the study.

Procedure

The procedure was the same as that in the preceding study except that "man" was substituted for "woman" in the written instructions. Since "man" may have a universal connotation, an additional sentence was inserted in the instructions: "We do not mean the concept of 'man' as in 'mankind' but the concept of 'man' meaning male."

Results

The same coding system was used as in the previous study, but as might be expected there were no instances of photos depicting some of the same categories. The reliability between a male and female coder ranged from .70 to 1.00.

The three statistically significant differences between genders were closeness (M_1 [male] = .00, M_2 [female] = .58, $F = 6.4$, $p < .01$); sports (M_1 [male] = .46, M_2 [female] = .16, $F = 3.88$, $p = .05$), and persons (M_1 [male] = .25, M_2 [female] = .67, $F = 5.34$, $p < .03$). Females show males more frequently as close and show photos involving persons when describing the meaning of "man," whereas males show more sports.

Again we have recourse to a hierarchy of orientations for males and females. These hierarchies are formed by listing first that category with the highest number of photos, second the next highest and so forth. The resulting hierarchy for males was (1) possessions, (2) work, (3) sports or recreation, (4) children, (5) persons, (6) aesthetics, (7) groups, (8) religion, and (9) closeness. For the females' photographic descriptions of "man," the hierarchy of categories was (1) persons, (2) closeness, (3) work, (4) possessions, (5) group, (6) children, (7) aesthetics, (8) sports, and (9) religion.

The greatest disparities for males' views pertain to "possessions" and "sports," which are ranked 1 and 3 for male subjects but 4 and 8 for females. The greatest disparities for the females' views pertain to "persons" and "closeness," ranked 1 and 2 for females but 5 and last for males. For males, "man" is associated with "possessions," "work," and "sports," but for females, "man" is associated with "persons" and "closeness."

Discussion

One of the best-known surveys of gender stereotypes was conducted by Broverman, Vogel, Broverman, Clarkson, and Rosenkrantz (1972). They asked college males and females to list characteristics on which adult males and females differed. The characteristics associated with men were related to competency, rationality, assertiveness, and toughness. The characteristics associated with women were warmth, compassion, and expressiveness.

The aforementioned study employing a questionnaire describes a very different set of information than the image-approach to meaning. To begin, it is necessary to differentiate the views of males and females by males and by females. In so doing, different categories of meaning emerge and very different interpretations are suggested. In the photo-meaning study, males are perceived by females as social, whereas males associate "man" with possessions, work, and sports (recreation).

In the questionnaire study, female is associated with sociability, but in the photo-association approach to meaning, female is associated with sociability and task orientation in the views of women, whereas males show a stereotypic view of the meaning of woman. In both image-meaning studies, an insider's view is afforded, and it contrasts with the meaning of the outsider because neither is afforded a view of the other in the other's context. Thus, each had little opportunity to perceive the psychological niche of the other. The result is conceptual conflict. The image-meaning approach described here presents an opportunity to explicate cognitive conflict and provides a visual process for improving understanding between groups that live in separate cognitive domains. The following study, which describes the meaning of "war" among children in two very separated countries, dramatizes this thesis.

The Meaning of War
in Germany and the United States[1]

It has been shown (Brehmen, 1976) that cognitive factors may produce conflict and that cognitive factors alone may cause prolonged disagreement, even in the absence of differences in interest or emotional factors. In the research reviewed by Brehmen, social judgments were the only cognitive variables considered. It is proposed here that a wide variety of social concepts are often critical to interpersonal and intergroup relations because of differences in the meaning of these concepts for persons or groups separated environmentally or politically. Thus in the two preceding studies differences in the personal constructs of males and females associated with the meaning of "woman" and "man" were proposed as the potential basis of gender conflict.

The Meaning of War and Peace
Among German and American Children

On the basis of the meaning of war and peace for the members of a given state, leaders may rise to power whose views of war and peace are consistent with those of the members of the state. On the same basis, priorities for state expenditures are determined and interstate actions and responses are influenced. For this reason, the meaning of war and peace has been explored extensively by social scientists (Cooper, 1965; Alvik, 1968; Rosell, 1968; Svancarova & Svancarova, 1967-1968, Haavedsrud, 1970). Most of these studies used verbal responses, although Svancarova and Svancarova used drawings as well as written notes. All the studies used children as subjects, assuming that they reflected adult views and that they were less influenced by social desirability. Only one of the studies (Cooper, 1965) compared the responses of children from different countries, but the results were descriptive and suggested no explanation for differences in English and Japanese students' perceptions of war and peace. It was noted, however, that older Japanese students were more vehement in their protest against war and more preoccupied with peace as an international movement.

In the study presented here differences in the orientations and personal constructs of children from Germany and the United States concerning the meaning of war and peace were explored.The children in Germany and the United States are separated geographically and experientially. Consistent with the self theory as a Environment-Self-Behavior system constituting a psychological niche, the environmental differences may be expected to be reflected in their self-concepts and personal constructs with regard to the stimulus words "war" and "peace." It is proposed that "war" is described in images of destruction more frequently in Germany than in the United States. It is further proposed that these differences in personal constructs derive from the agency of different self-concepts in the "war"-"peace" environment and in this context poses serious political implications.

The study described here proposes that German in comparison with American children associate war with destruction more frequently. In the United States, war is distal, and the citizens are observers. In Germany war is proximal and citizens are suffering participants.

Almost all German citizens only one generation removed suffered the death of friends and relatives and the devastation and horrors of war. Today Germany is divided, and immediate threats of war persist. Indeed, according to a survey conducted in July 1981, 17% of a sample of German adults reported that they sometimes dream about the war (Sauun, 1983, p. 22).

In the United States, on the other hand, war is remote. The major effects of war are limited to the military; life is not changed drastically for most of the citizens who are not associated with the military. Moreover, wars in recent times have been waged in some distant land. Consequently, there is an air of unreality about war in the United States. War is known, but it is not understood because it is not usually personal. In addition to examining the meaning of war, differences will be explored between American and German children as to the meaning of peace to help clarify the proposed differences in the meaning of war since, in a dialectical sense, war and peace define each other.

In contrast to earlier studies, photo-communication was emphasized in order to avoid problems of language translation. As in the earlier studies cited, it was assumed that understanding of adult views can be developed by investigating the perceptions of their children.

Subjects

The subjects of the study were 40 female and 40 male fourth-graders attending public schools in Orlando and Winter Park, Florida, as well as in Bremerhaven, West Germany. All the children were between the ages of 8 years and 10 months and 10 years and 11 months. Two elementary schools representing all socioeconomic status (SES) levels were selected from each city. In all cases the parents' country of birth was the same as the country of study. Only one child in all the classrooms of either country refused to participate in the study. This child was replaced by another volunteer.

Equipment

Each subject was provided with a Polaroid camera with a built-in flash and loaded with film. The subjects were instructed in its use.

Procedure

The following instructions for taking photographs were read to the children in their respective languages. The German directions were back-translated to assure the reliability of the instructions.

> Good morning (or good afternoon), I am Mrs. Dinklage. I would like to find out what American and German children think of war and peace. I would like to ask you to take two photos for me, one photo representing war and one photo representing peace. Take the photos of anything that comes to your mind when you think of war or peace. You may even decide to build something and take a photo of it. Whatever you do, it is entirely up to you. The photos do not have to be perfect, and there are no good or bad photos. Make sure you do not tell anyone about your ideas. Keep it a secret. When you have finished, I will show you similar photos taken by (German or American) children. Please bring the photos tomorrow, and do not forget to return the camera.

When the students returned the photographs, a focused, structured interview was conducted consisting of three questions: (1) Which of the two photos represents peace and which represents war? (2) What does this photo mean to you (relating to war)? (3) What does this photo mean to you (relating to peace)? All phases of the data collection were conducted by Dinklage who is multilingual, German being her native language.

Content Analysis

The coding categories were derived, in part, from earlier research previously cited with regard to the meaning of war and peace for children, and on the basis of inspection of photographs from a pilot study involving eight German and seven American children in schools in Germany and the United States.

The categories of war included: (1) armaments—ships, weapons, or symbols of armaments, (2) consequences of war—a person or persons or representations of person(s), who have been injured or killed because of war, (3) destruction—a photograph, drawing, or picture that shows a home or house or anything that represents a home, such as a doll-house, which is either destroyed or deserted, or dead trees, (4) human—person(s) who are fighting or shooting, or show a weapon, and (5) other—a photograph that is ambivalent as to the content or not clear and does not fall into any of the above categories.

The categories of peace included: (1) animals—a photograph showing an animal, (2) human—a person or persons or something representing a person or persons, (3) nature—a photograph showing flower(s) and/or tree(s), (4) sanctuary—a place, such as a house or church, where a person would feel safe from external environmental conditions; signs of peace, such as the Bible, and (5) other—a photograph which is ambivalent as to content or not clear and does not fall into any of the above categories.

Two American school psychologists who were uninformed about the nature of the study were asked to sort all pictorial representations of war and peace into the prescribed categories. After completing the sorting process, the coders were given the children's responses or translated responses to the three open-ended questions asking the children to explain their photographs. The coders then recategorized any photographs that were, in their judgment, misplaced on the first sorting. For example, one photograph taken by a German child was not sufficiently clear as to content, but was described by the student in the interview in these terms: "After the war, everything is destroyed, dead people, few survivors." The photograph was subsequently recategorized from "other" to "consequences of war."

Interrater reliability for the pictorial representations of war and peace were .94. Interrater reliability for the pictorial representations plus the children's verbal responses was .96 (see Figures 3.3 and 3.4).

Figure 3.3. The meaning of "war" (photography by German child).

Results

Chi-square analysis revealed no relationship between the child's nationality and the five categories of the pictorial representation of war (X^2 (4) = 2.62, *ns*). However, when each of the five categories was considered by itself by means of the z-statistic, a significant difference was found between the proportions of American and German children selecting the category "other" (z = 2.06, $p < .05$). Significantly more American children furnished pictorial representations of war which were placed in the "other" category.

Consistent with the original hypothesis more photographs taken by (German children) were coded as "destruction," but the difference was not statistically significant (13 versus 8, see Table 3.1).

However, when the pictorial representations plus the verbal responses about war were analyzed, a significant association was found between the child's nationality and the five categories (X^2 (4) = 11.70, $p < .05$). Furthermore, when each of the five categories was considered by itself, the z-statistic showed significant differences between the proportion of American and German children selecting the categories "destruction" (z = 1.98, $p < .05$), "consequences of war" (z = 2.42, $p < .05$), and "other" (z = 2.42, $p < .01$). Significantly more German children furnished pictorial representations plus verbal responses of war which were coded as "destruction" or "consequences of war," whereas significantly more American children's responses were coded as "other" (see Table 3.1).

Similar analyses were conducted with regard to the meaning of peace (see Table 3.2). Again, chi-square analysis showed no significant association (X^2 (4) = 4.70, p > .05). However, when each of the five categories was considered by itself by means of the z-statistic, a significant difference was found between the proportion of American and German children selecting the categories "human" (z = 2.39, $p < .05$) and "nature" (z = 2.60, $p < .01$). Significantly more

Figure 3.4. The meaning of ''war'' (photograph by an American child.

TABLE 3.1: War: Pictorial Representations and Pictorial Representations Plus Verbal Responses

Nationality	Pictorial		Pictorial & Verbal	
	U.S.	Germany	U.S.	Germany
Destruction	8	13	4*	9*
Human	9	9	12	10
Armaments	12	14	12	14
Consequences of war	0	0	2*	7*
Other	8*	4*	7**	0**
Total	37	40	37	40

*$p < .05$; **$p < .01$
X^2 (4) (Pictorial) = 2.62, $p > .05$.
X^2 (4) (Pictorial & Verbal) = 11.70, $p < .05$.
Note: Three of the American children did not submit a photograph concerning war. In one case the child explained that she wanted to take a photograph of her dog and cat fighting, but she was not able to make them fight.

American children furnished pictorial representations of peace which were placed into the "nature" category, whereas significantly more German children supplied pictorial representations of peace which were placed into the "human" category (see Table 3.2).

Similar analyses involving the pictorial representations plus verbal responses about peace were not statistically significant (X^2 (4) = 5.34, $p > .05$). Furthermore, none of the five categories considered separately by means of the z-statistic were significant (see Table 3.2).

Discussion

The results of the examination of the meaning of war and of peace for German and American children indicate that for German children war is more frequently associated with images of destruction of property, injury, or death. Moreover, for German children, peace is more frequently associated with images of people. Consistent with the initial hypotheses, German children, in fact, hold a very different view of war. War is perceived more frequently by German children as being destructive.

TABLE 3.2: Peace: Pictorial Representations and Pictorial Representations Plus Verbal Responses

Nationality	Pictorial		Pictorial & Verbal	
	U.S.	Germany	U.S.	Germany
Sanctuary	5	6	5	7
Human	14*	22*	15	22
Animals	8	6	8	5
Nature	10**	4**	10	6
Other	2	2	0	0
Total	39	40	39	40

*$p < .05$; **$p < .01$

X^2 (4) (Pictorial) = 4.70, $p > .05$.

X^2 (4) (Pictorial & Verbal) = 5.34, $p < .05$.

In their entirety, however, the results may be extrapolated (albeit cautiously due to nonsignificance of the results regarding the analysis of the photographs without the focused interviews) to suggest that for German children, and perhaps German adults, war is more personally threatening. It involves people, people whose lives are threatened, and the people referred to include themselves, their families, and friends. On the basis of broad inference, this immediate association of war as a threat to the self is less likely among Americans because war for Americans is remote, has a character of unreality, and has had a low probability of affecting continuity of life.

The study underscores the relationship between meaning and environment and the resulting potential for cognitive conflict between groups in different environments. The meaning of war is different between two countries where in one country the view is that of a distant observer, whereas in the other country the view is that of a participant. The differences in the meaning of war may have implications for differences in approaches to international conflict and how leaders of different countries might address international issues in their efforts to seek the support of their constituents.

The marked differences in the meaning of critical concepts between groups of persons separated and enveloped in different environments is proposed as the fundamental origin of misunderstanding and conflict leading to further separation and the spiraling of the conflict effect. Previous research by Tajfel (1970) has suggested that separation of persons into two groups is associated with group-centrism (exclusive support within groups) leading to conflict between groups. The present study offers an extension of the theory of conflict and proposes that separation of groups leads to the development of different meanings for crucial concepts which derive from different self-concepts, followed by increased stress, separation, and conflict. The crucial concern is the difference in the meaning of critical concepts which are rendered intractable because the parties are unaware of the nature of the deep-seated differences. Indeed, explicating the differences in meaning through photo-communication may begin the process of inter-group understanding. Revelation of personal constructs or the meaning of crucial concepts between groups in conflict is assumed to be an initial step toward intergroup understanding.

Overview

The three studies described here have their origins in the assumption that the meaning of crucial concepts, including the concept of "self," emanates from the agency of the self theory in interacting with the environment. Thus by examining these personally constructed meanings of "man," "woman," "war," and "peace," an extended theory of the self may be inferred. The theory of the self is a general theory presumed to be involved in every aspect of human behavior, processing of information, and emotion. The theory of the self functions as a control, mediating the environment and behavior, and all efforts to understand human behavior must first attempt to understand the self in interaction with the person's environment. Previous approaches to the study the self have limited the parameters by the nature of the circumscribed question and by excluding environmental variables. The result has been to limit the utility of self theory because of ecological invalidity.

In the present more inclusive approach to the study of the self, where the meaning of personally significant concepts were examined, the results demonstrate that the self theory and the associated personal constructs derive, in part, from the gender and national environment. It was proposed that the resulting differences in the meaning of critical concepts for males and females as well as for German and American children may be the basis of conflicts which elude resolution because their origins are in the very self-concepts and orientations of the participants, who are unaware of basis of disagreement. Finally, it was proposed that the differences in meaning of critical concepts derive from the separation of the opposing groups, and that the misunderstanding of cognitive differences may be clarified by pictorial displays of the meaning of critical concepts. In effect, the opposing groups reverse roles by viewing the world, or at least some critical concepts, as viewed by the other.

The next chapter extends the study of environmental influences on the theory of the self by examining the meaning of "the good life" in the United States and Poland. Again, as in this chapter, it will be shown that the self concept is influenced by the cultural environment. It is proposed that differences in cultural environment are associated with differences in orientations and self-concepts which may be the basis of profound conflict.

Note

1. This is an abbreviated account of an article by Dinklage & Ziller (1989).

CHAPTER
4

The Self and Value Orientations:
The Iconic Communication of
Values Across Cultures

In the earlier chapters, the theory of the self was described through orientations or personal constructions in the environment in relation to the meaning of critical concepts such as "self," "man" or "woman," "war" or "peace." In the process, gender, personal history, and even nation history were demonstrated to be inextricably involved in the theory of the self. Obviously, the meaning of a large number of additional concepts such as "work" or "life," which necessarily redounds to the meaning of the self, could be examined. It is assumed here that presenting diverse concepts for photo explication and interpretation will afford the most complete construction of the self theory. Thus, the present chapter expands the inquiry into the region of values as they relate to the self by examining the meaning of "the good life." Values are assumed to be a cardinal concept for evoking self-environment interactions.

Selecting a conception of "value" has been a critical issue in axiology as well as in the disciplines of psychology and sociology, which have examined the concept empirically. Typically, the term has been used to refer to selective or choice behavior with respect to physical, social, or ideal objects (Smith, 1969), but definitions of value are as diverse as their disciplinary origins. Still, the concept is central to the social sciences.

Bandura (1977) has noted that personality theories tend to explain variations in behavior in terms of differences in values, but they cannot predict how values will regulate behavior. That measures of values are often observed to be highly discrepant with or even contrary to behavior in everyday settings casts serious doubt on the possibility of generalizing from survey-based data to nonsurvey situations. One likely explanation for this discrepancy is that values are typically conceived in terms of preferability rather than preference. Preference is an existential proposition. It

AUTHOR'S NOTE: This is an abbreviated account of an article by Rorer & Ziller (1982) in the *Journal of Cross-Cultural Psychology, 13,* 352-361. Copyright Western Washington State College. Reprinted by permission of Sage Publications, Inc.

concerns a comparative evaluation of concrete alternatives available for selection (Morris, 1946). Preferability, on the other hand, refers to normative standards for selection (what ought to be selected) or ideal preferences (Rokeach, 1973).

If values are conceived in terms of preferability it is unlikely that selective behavior in the everyday environment will provide an external verification for subscription to those values. When the environment does not afford alternatives of selection that fall within the realm of preferability or the ideal, or if the individual has not adopted normative standards, then personal standards will guide selection.

To study the behavioral component of values, the discrepancies between values and the alternatives of choice in the environment, and between normative standards and individual preferences, must be recognized. At this level of analysis values may be viewed as abstract predilections that provide orientations, with the self as the point of reference, to the preferred social and physical objects comprising the environment. In this sense universalism of objects is a prerequisite of universalism of value components.

The universe of objects (the components of value orientations) is determinate and will, in part, determine the range of orientations. An interesting question, and one that prompted the present research, involves the relationship between complexity of the environment and the range of value orientations. Complexity of environment refers to the degree of differentiation or the number of component parts. A complex environment is highly differentiated and offers a broader range of alternatives of selection than the simplex environment. For example, it has been demonstrated (Ziller, Vera, & Santoya, 1989) that affluent children in comparison with children of poverty used a broader range of orientations in photographically answering the question "Who am I?" Presumably, the children from an affluent environment are provided with a broader range of alternatives than the children from an impoverished environment. The universalism of value components must be viewed in this context, with congruity of component objects as a necessary condition. Some degree of universalism between any two cultures can be expected because of objects common to each (e.g., food, art, social, interactions), with the highest degree of universalism between the cultures with the most congruent set and range of objects.

The present study of value orientations breaks new ground in value theory by employing photography, allowing subjects to respond freely to preferred social and physical objects in the environment. The participants were given a loaded camera and asked photographically to depict "the good life." Morris (1946), Rescher (1969), and Reisman (1958) have suggested that values may be operationalized through the individual's description of "the good life." The resulting unobtrusive approach is creative rather than reactive, and since responses present person-environment transactions, the procedure is sensitive to the actual conditions of life. Finally, photo-communication is universal language which facilitates cross-cultural studies.

Through this free-response format the number of components comprising the value orientations of American and Polish college freshmen was examined, and a comparison of these components was conducted to test empirically the previously assumed concept of universalism. Polish subjects were selected to compare to American subjects because of the differences between the two cultures in political ideologies, economic conditions, and the historical instability of Poland relative to that of the United States. However, the two countries are comparable in terms of being industrialized, Western cultures. Data were collected from Polish subjects by the author at Adam Mickiewicz University in Poznan. Data collection was completed in the weeks preceding the initial workers' strikes in the summer of 1980.

Subjects

The American participants were 40 University of Florida introductory psychology students who partially fulfilled a course requirement by participating in the study. The 20 males and 20 females were all 18 years of age and were either first- or second-quarter freshmen. The Polish students (18 males and 18 females) were incoming freshmen 17- to 18-years-old who were contacted through faculty members at Adam Mickiewicz University.

Procedure

American subjects received the following instructions:

> We want you to take three photographs that best describe the good life from your point of view. These photographs may be of anything as long as they tell something about what the good life is to you. Before you begin, it will be helpful to think about the photographs you would like to take. You should not be interested in your skill as a photographer, but only in your photographic description of the good life.

A Polish-language equivalent of the good life was derived through a joint translation by an American fluent in Polish and a Pole fluent in English. The translation was later back-translated by a different English-speaking Pole and Polish-speaking American. In the back-translation the instructions were the same except that the good life was replaced by "what the good things in life are to you." Written instructions were also included for the use of a camera.

Subjects were given a 110-mm Keystone Instamatic pocket camera with a built-in flash. The photographs were not developed until after they were turned in, in an effort to ensure anonymity of response. Subjects received the cameras on a Thursday and were asked to return them the following Tuesday so as to allow photographs to be taken over the weekend. Additional time was allowed for the completion of the task on request.

As a result of earlier research and blind inspection of all the photographs in the present study, the following categories were used to code the sets of photographs: (1) children, (2) recreational activities (actual participation or equipment), (3) nudes, (4) cars, (5) stereos, (6) food, (7) school (books or study activity), (8) religion (church or religious objects), (9) groups of three or more, (10) single persons of the opposite sex or male-female dyads, (11) private residences, (12) alcoholic beverages, (13) hedonic tone, (14) aesthetic orientation, and (15) range of orientations.

Two independent raters coded each set of photographs. Interrater reliability ranged from .79 to 1.00 (see Figures 4.1 and 4.2).

Results

A 2×2 analysis of variance by culture and sex of subject was conducted with reference to the presence of photographs coded according to each of the value orientations. Americans, in contrast to Poles, included significantly more photographs pertaining to recreation ($F(1, 72) = 7.80$, $p <$ .007), stereos ($F(1, 72) = 5.80$, $p < .01$), single persons of the opposite sex and males-females dyads ($Y(1, 72) = 3.93$, $p < .05$), hedonic tone ($F(1.72) = 13.44$. $p < .0005$), and range of orientations ($F(1.72) = 9.29$, $p < .003$).

Poles, on the other hand, included significantly more photographs pertaining to children ($F(1, 72) = 33.53$, $p <$ .0001), school ($F(1, 72) = 5.64$, $p < .02$), private residences ($F(1, 72) = 3.41$, $p < .06$), and religion ($F(1, 72) = 8.86$. $p < .004$).

Females presented significantly more photographs pertaining to aesthetic orientation ($F(1, 72) = 7.61$, $p < .007$), groups ($F(1, 72) = 3.82$, $p < .005$), and food ($F(1, 72) = 4.10$, $p < .04$). American males included more photographs of nudes ($F(1, 72) = 9.29$, $p < .003$).

Discussion

In this study the previously assumed universalism of value components was empirically tested in a free-response manner in the context of the transactional relationship between the subject's environment as a set of social and physical objects, and values as selective orientations toward those ob-

Figure 4.1. The meaning of "the good life" (photographs by a Polish student).

103

Figure 4.2. The meaning of "the good life" (photographs by an American student).

jects. It was hypothesized that the range of value orientations of Polish subjects would be lower than the range of orientations of American subjects. The obtained results leave little doubt that American subjects presented a broader range of selective orientations. The mean number of categories coded per set for American subjects was 4.14 as compared to 2.65 for Polish subjects.

Of particular interest are the results with regard to stereos, nudes, and children. It was observed that while stereos were common to the American subjects' photographs and nudes were prevalent in the photographs of American males, neither of these categories was represented in the photographs of Polish subjects. The objects are not common to the Polish environment, and this may well account for the differences. With regard to children, it was observed that none of the American males, and only one American female, presented a photograph pertaining to this category. This result may also be interpreted in terms of the uncommonness of children in the environment of American college freshmen.

The major distinction between the Polish and American subjects is along the dimension of privatistic versus institutional orientations. The results for American subjects display a similar pattern to previous studies of American college freshmen, which depicted them as being primarily concerned with private values as distinguished from traditional normative values (Katz, 1968; Jacob, 1957; Trent & Craise, 1967). The Polish subjects, on the other hand, were more oriented toward the social institutions of education, church, and family (as indicated by photographs pertaining to private residences and children), which are characteristic values of Polish national culture (Szczepanski, 1970). The institutional orientation of the Pole suggests an orientation toward enduring sources of life satisfactions. Such enduring sources are likely to be particularly significant in a country marked by change and instability. Indeed, family, church, and education are among the few enduring characteristics of Poland's history.

More significantly, however, the results show differences in the self-concepts of citizens from the different nations. As noted at the outset of this chapter, the orientations of the subjects with regard to the environment in terms of "the good life" are presumed to emanate from the theory of the self. The self theory of Poles was associated with institutional orientations (family, education, church), whereas Americans were more oriented toward private values. These differences in the self-concepts of the two groups appear only when we present the question of "the good life" and view the resulting personal constructs which are developed within the different environments. As a result of studying orientations with regard to values, critical facets of the self are portrayed.

Chapters 3 and 4 have described how categorization of the self within a group or a nation alters the orientations of the members. These alterations in orientation derive from the presentation of different environments in interaction with the self theory. Again these differences were elicited through the presentation of poignant questions concerning the meaning of crucial concepts. The next chapter extends the inquiry of the development of a personal theory of the self when the person is required to respond to the social environment where others are mirrors to the self and present information about the self. Toward what do we orient when others present their images of ourselves, and how does this reflect on the self theory? In the next two chapters, the insider's and outsider's view of the self will be examined in terms of symbolic interaction (Mead, 1934; Stryker, 1980).

CHAPTER
5

Self and Others' View
of Self and Country

The previous chapters have focused almost entirely on insider's observations, the view of the self as depicted by the self. This egocentric picture, however, denies the interaction of the self with the social environment. The self is seen as encapsulated within itself, contrary to Cooley's (1918) observation that we are "each to each a looking glass that doth pass." This chapter then considers the interaction of the insider's and outsider's views of the self and of the United States. At the base is symbolic interaction theory (Mead, 1934; Stryker, 1980), which here is assimilated within the Environment-Self-Behavior psychological niche.

The relationship between the self and other is one of the most exquisite theoretical issues in the social sciences. What is the confluence of self and other? How does the other influence the self, and the self influence the other? How are the self and other viewed by external and internal observers? At the base is symbolic interaction theory. The problem area is described in a variety of ways but in general is concerned with the "reciprocity of society and individual." In examining this process the external observer brings explanatory models to the subjective experiences and performances of those being observed (Martindale, 1960; Stryker & Statham, 1985). Thus, symbolic interaction is concerned with the reciprocal influence of persons who as they act take into account one another's characteristics. The process is continuous. Consistent with the Environment-Self-Behavior theory presented here, it is noted that in this process, the individual (the self) is active and creative rather than simply responsive to outside forces. The self develops in response to others' responses to the self, but, at once, controls the responses of others.

In the first experiment described here, the nature of the interaction between the self and other is demonstrated through the exchange of inside and outside images of the self, using the photographic self-concept. It is proposed that

AUTHORS' NOTE: This is a much-abbreviated description of an unpublished report by Ziller, Okura, & Burns (1989).

the self theory of the individual is associated with the extent to which the individual has recourse to social sources of information concerning the self. Those with the more permeable self-concepts will accept more information about the self from others. Thus it is proposed that persons with more complex and more socially oriented self-concepts assimilate more information from others about the self. Or more generally, interaction effects between the self and the social environment are more pronounced for the more complex and more socially oriented persons.

Subjects

Twenty-nine students enrolled in an introductory social psychology class participated in the study. Fourteen were males and 15 were females. Participation was voluntary.

Personality Measures

Three components of the self-concept which were assumed to be associated with assimilation of self-feedback served as the independent variables: self-esteem, self-complexity, social openness. The measures derive from social schemas of self and others (Ziller, 1973).

The index of self-esteem is derived from six nonverbal items which present the subject with a horizontal array of circles and a list of significant others including the self. The person is asked to assign each person to a circle in the horizontal array. In accordance with the cultural norm, positions more to the left are associated with higher self-esteem. The item score is the weighted position of the self in the six items. Lower self-esteem is related to social responsiveness (Ziller, 1973).

Social openness pertains to the individual's orientation toward seeking association with others. The person is asked to draw as many or as few lines as he/she wishes from the circle representing the self to the circles representing other people. The item score is simply the number of lines connecting the self with others. The greater the number of lines, the higher the social openness score. Previous research has shown that openness is heavily weighted with regard to sociability (Ziller, 1973).

The measure of self-complexity is the number of adjectives from a list of 109 that the person checks as a description of the self. The greater the number of adjectives checked, the greater the self-complexity. As noted earlier, self-complexity is an index of self-differentiation. Previous research has shown that persons with higher scores search for more information before reaching a decision, are more widely chosen by others as friends, and identify with a wider range of others (Ziller, Martel, & Morrison, 1977).

Procedure

After completing the social schemas tasks, the subject was presented with the following instructions (and a question about the length of time they had known their friend):

> We would like to know how you see *yourself*, i.e., how you perceive yourself. One method which communicates how people see themselves is to have them take photographs. We would like you to take 6 photographs that communicate who you are according to how you see yourself. We are not concerned with your photographic skill, only with how you see yourself. Since some pictures may not turn out, please write down what you have photographed. Since there are no flashbulbs, take photographs in well-lighted places. Since we will be asking you to take some more photographs, please keep the unfinished roll of film in the camera. Remember, take photographs of anything that communications who you are.

An Instamatic camera and a 12-exposure roll of film were given to the subjects. After the subjects had completed the photographs, they were told to give the following set of instructions to the same-sex friend who knew them best:

> We would like to know how you see (subject's name), that is, how you perceive this person. One method which communicates how people see others is to have them take photographs. We would like you to take 6 photographs that communicate who this person is. These photographs can be of anything just as long as they com-

municate who this person is. We are not concerned with your photographic ability, but only how you see this other person. Since some pictures may not turn out, please write down what you have photographed. Since there are no flashbulbs, take the photographs in well-lighted places. When you have finished, please return the undeveloped roll of film and your list to the other person who you have photographed. He/she will return them to us. Remember, take photographs of anything that communicates who you think (subject's name) is.

Subjects were asked to try not to influence what their friends photographed in any way. When the film was developed, the subjects were given the final instructions:

We would like you to look at the photographs that you and your friend have taken. During the next few minutes, select the 6 photographs among the entire 12 that you feel best communicate who you are. The photographs that you select can be any combination of those taken by yourself and your friend. After you have chosen the 6 photographs, place a number on the back of each which indicates the order in which the photographs best communicate who you are. Start with number 1 and proceed until number 6. In addition, indicate whether the photograph was taken by yourself or your friend.

Upon completion of the selection procedure, subjects were asked to fill out a brief questionnaire. The questionnaire consisted of two items: (1) Before asking your friend to take the photographs, how well did you think your friend knew you? The response continuum for these item was in the form of very well, well, fairly well, and not well at all.

The criterion was the photographs which were taken by the friend as representative of the self. The six selected photographs were ranked; the sum of the ranks of the photographs taken by the friend represented the score.

Results

The correlation between self-complexity and the sum of weighted photographs by the other was $-.37$ ($n = 28$, $p < .05$), and between social openness and sum of the weighted photographs was $-.45$ ($p < .05$). The correlation for self-esteem was not significant ($r = .01$).

Discussion

The results show that responsiveness to information from others about the self is related to personal factors. The more complex and more socially oriented persons accept more photographs from others when there is opportunity for an outside view of the self. Thus, self-definition results from an interaction of the self and other, a combination of the inside view of the self (personal) and outside view of the self (social), but the degree of interaction is a variable in and of itself. In this regard, the results suggest that the origins of the more complex personality may be the nature of their interaction with a variety of other persons. The more complex persons are presumed to have contact with a more diverse group of persons and are presented with more information concerning their own identity, but what is more, they assimilate that information.

Again, the unique characteristics of photo-communication permit a more direct exchange of information by avoiding at least one step in the coding of verbal descriptions of images and another in the decoding of verbal descriptions of images. In addition, the presence of the communicator is eliminated, rendering the event more personal, and perhaps increasing the potential impact of the information.

More generally, the use of feedback about the self from an outsider using photo-communication presents a threshold for a world of ideas. The following study expands the approach used with images of persons to images of countries.

International Perception:
Insiders' Versus Outsiders' Views
of the United States

The purpose of this second study was to investigate national perception of the United States through photo-communication by insiders (Americans) versus outsiders (Japanese, Taiwanese, and Venezuelans). Selltiz et al. (1963) found that foreign students' views of the United States (while studying in the United States) were very much influenced by their national and cultural background, or what has been referred to as reflectivity or personal biases of the outside observer (Collier & Collier, 1986). In some sense, with regard to international perception, the outsiders have a basis of comparison, their own nation. The insiders do not usually have recourse to similar experiences in another nation, so their judgment is absolute or perhaps develops in comparison with some other nation, which the political leaders use for comparison and contrast. In any case, simply because of differences in potential for comparison, the insider and outsider views may be expected to be divergent and reflect on the self-concepts of the perceivers or orienters. How then do self and others view the self-related nation? What are the potential effects on self-nation perception of bi-national vision?

All earlier research on international perception relied on questionnaires. In the present study, again the photo-communication approach was applied, thereby minimizing differences in verbal communications between outsiders and insiders from different nations using different languages. In a real sense, images are the universal language.

Subjects

The participants were 30 American students (10 men and 20 women), 19 Japanese students (7 men and 12 women), 31 Taiwanese students (19 men and 10 woman, 2 did not report gender), and 15 Venezuelan students (7 men and 8 women). The distribution of majors for the 95 subjects clustered in the Liberal Arts and Sciences, and Engineering. The Japanese and Taiwanese students were somewhat older than the rest. Most of the foreign students had been in the United States for more than two years. All were enrolled at the University of Florida, and all were volunteers who were contacted through the foreign student office. The Americans were volunteers from two psychology classes.

Equipment

A Concord pocket camera with a built-in flash loaded with a 24-exposure film cartridge was used. The camera did not require focusing.

Procedure

The following directions were presented to the participants.

> We are using photography to try to improve understanding between people. To do this we need a wide variety of people. We want you to take four photographs that best describe "what the United States means to me as reflected in life in Gainesville." These photographs may be of anything, as long as they tell something about what the United States means to you. When you have finished taking each photograph, describe in six words or less what the photographs are intended to portray, using the space indicated on the page.

The instructions were not translated for foreign students because they all possessed the ability to understand the English instructions.

Coding

In the first stage, the photographs were coded independently by two coders in terms of 27 categories which were developed on the basis of the categories used in our earlier research as well as Wagner's (1979) photographic interviewing study of a planned community where he presented the participants with 17 photographs showing various community reference points. These categories were extended, however, to include categories emerging from an overall inspection of all the photographs made in response to these special instructions (which included the requirement of a six-word description of the content of the photographs by the subject) and for these special subjects. Then, using descriptions of photographs provided by the subjects, the categories were further extended and refined to make up the final 27. Coding reliability between two raters ranged from .37 to .90.

The Analysis of Content

The 27 resulting but not exhaustive categories included: (1) group—photographs which include more than two persons; (2) aesthetic orientations—photographs focusing upon one or more of the following: plants, trees, sky, scenery, painting, sculpture, or porcelain; (3) religious orientations—photographs showing at least one religious symbol such as church, Christian cross, altar, statue of a religious person, or religious book; (4) sports—photographs showing some kind of sports-related activities; (5) entertainment—photographs showing game machines, television sets, musical shows; (6) cars—photographs showing cars; (7) communications—photographs showing communications activities, communications devices like telephones, magazines, newspapers; (8) patriotism—photographs showing the national flag or patriotic items; (9) technological orientations—photographs including computers or advanced scientific machines; (10) money—photographs including money or items indicating money; (11) food—photographs including food, restaurants, or grocery stores; (12) education—photographs including libraries, study desks, or objects indicating education; (13) development—photographs showing buildings, grounds under construction, or items indicating the building process; (14) freedom—photographs including church, people debating, political posters, or objects indicating freedom as described in the subjects' comments; (15) University of Florida—photographs showing the University of Florida campus; (16) equality—photographs showing women or members of a minority group described by the subject in photo-interviews as depicting equality; (17) individualism—photographs showing a lonely person or a conspicuously single individual as indicated by the subjects' comments;

(18) poverty—photographs which include low-income housing or a poor section of the town; (19) security—photographs showing a police station as observed during photo-assisted interviews; (20) roads—photographs showing highways, road signals, or roads; (21) democracy—photographs including protesters or scenes of discussion group as observed during photo-assisted interviews; (22) luxury—photographs including luxurious cars or expensive homes; (23) love or friendship—photographs showing persons hugging each other or smiling at each other; (24) melting pot—photographs including mixed-race groups; (25) environment abuse—photographs showing trash cans, waste on the road or in a stream or lake; (26) confusion—photographs showing graffiti on the wall and the negative connotation as commented upon by the subjects during photo-assisted interviews; (27) enormity—photographs including buildings, cars, scenery described as massive by the subjects. Figures 5.1 and 5.2 show photos taken by a foreigner and an American, respectively.

Comparisons Between the United States and Other Nations Combined

In this analysis, the Americans were compared with the other three national groups combined in order to focus on inside versus outside views. Here the Bonferroni t-test was used because of its rigid control over the accumulation of error or probability under conditions of a large number of t-tests.

Sports ($p = .0518$), patriotism ($p = .0321$), food ($p = .0093$), development ($p = .0514$), freedom ($p = .0095$), and security ($p = .0346$) were the categories which were statistically significant (see Table 5.1). The Bonferroni t-test revealed that Americans in comparison with other nationals showed fewer photos pertaining to "sports," "food," and "security" but more photos pertaining to "patriotism," "development," and "freedom."

Figure 5.1. What "the United States" means (photographs by a Taiwanese student).

Figure 5.2. What "the United States" means (photographs by an American student).

TABLE 5.1: **Mean Percentage of Photographs Taken by Americans, Japanese, Taiwanese, and Venezuelans in Six Statistically Significant Categories**

	Culture			
	American (n = 30)	Japanese (n = 19)	Taiwanese (n = 31)	Venezuelan (n = 15)
Sports	1.66	3.94	6.45	8.33
Patriotism	7.50	2.63	0.80	5.00
Food	1.66	5.26	11.29	8.33
Development	8.33	2.63	0.80	6.66
Freedom	21.66	13.15	12.09	8.33
Security	0.00	0.00	1.61	6.66

Discussion

The results are interpreted in terms of the differences in bases for judgment between the insiders versus the outsiders. The outsiders from Taiwan, Japan, and Venezuela have their own nations with which to compare and contrast images, and those images that are selected are salient according to their basis of comparison. Thus, outsiders are more oriented toward food and sports, both of which are in greater display in the United States than in the comparison nations.

The insiders, on the other hand, are compelled to find a basis for judgment in the form of some nations that are used in the educational and political institutions to establish nation identity, or they may simply have recourse to descriptions of the United States presented in the educational institutions that socialize the students with regard to national identity through a combination of stereotypic descriptions and contrasts with a foreign country selected for its perceived antipodal differences. Thus, Russia before 1989 may have served as a basis of comparison.

American students were found to orient toward patriotism, freedom, and development. Unfortunately, this rather stereotypic self-nation view of the United States cannot be compared with the outsiders' views of their respective nation, but the possibility is intriguing.

What is apparent is that the outsiders are perceiving the United States somewhat differently than the insiders, and the bi-national vision, if you will, offers an opportunity for symbolic interaction. Indeed, the combination of the insiders' and outsiders' views presents a somewhat different overall perspective. It would be interesting to employ a procedure similar to that in the first study to examine how different national groups might integrate outsiders' views, and what views would prevail.

Consistent with the theory of the self and the psychological niche, it is also proposed that these orientations must be considered as revelations of the self-concept of the perceiver. Freedom, patriotism, and development tend to be more associated with the meaning of the American self. Again, as in the earlier study of the meaning of "the good life" in the United States and Poland, national identity and the self-concept are related. This is not to raise the question of national character. It is proposed, however, that members with different national environments are differentially oriented, which in turn derives from differences in self-perceptions.

Overview

The two studies described here emanate from the symbolic interaction framework which emphasizes the interplay between the self and the other. In these studies the interplay involved differences in orientations between insiders and outsiders as they described through photo-images the "self" and "the United States." The approach acknowledges the influence of the social environment on the perceptions of the insiders, and in the first study demonstrates that the influence varies in terms of the self-concept of the perceiver. Person-environment interaction must take into account the views of others in the environment. The use of photo-communication in this process of self-other revelation makes possible the utilization of the views of other groups of persons, where both self and other might benefit from an exchange of views of critical concepts. These include parents and their children's views of "the good life" or the meaning of "the city of Gainesville" by Gainesville citizens of different ages. Through photographic images the contrasting orientations of the different groups may be compared and the differences in orientation and meaning discussed in order to improve understanding through the educative process of conflict and reconceptualization, including the reconceptualization of the self.

In this chapter I have tried to demonstrate the significance of the interaction of the views of the insider and outsider with regard to the self-concept. Essentially this is simply a special case of self-environment interaction where the environment involves the perceptions of the self by the other. The next chapter extends this inquiry of person-environment interaction to the topic of person-event interaction. Again, however, the events examined are entirely social in nature.

CHAPTER

6

The Meaning of Life Events:
An Insider's Extemporaneous View

In the following studies, the investigator capitalizes on the very special characteristic of the camera to record events instantly as they take place and where they take place. Furthermore, if the actors themselves take the photographs, we may observe self-event interaction in situ without interference from a third party. The events described here include divorce, release from prison, pre-marriage and post-marriage decision, and the social encounter between a man in a wheelchair and a crowd. Again, the orientations of the actor are recorded photographically by the actor, and these orientations are analyzed in an effort to understand the actor's psychological niche under conditions of social intensity. In contrast to most of the earlier studies, however, the sets of photographs were discussed at length with the actors in what might be called photo-assisted interviews.

Experience of an event is defined as "any occurrence, behavioral or environmental—of which we are aware or which has stood out as figure" (Levy, 1963). Certain adult experiences are of crucial concern because they may serve as a *rite de passage* for other experiences. Accompanying the experience are expectations of the significance of the experience by the subject as well as by others.

Most crucial experiences are social in nature. The experience usually involves the self in contact with significant others, and the emergent concept of the social self acts as a guide to future behaviors. Thus, if a situation can be devised to observe the subject from the inside out during the course of an event, the self-event interaction observation should show orientations and aspects of the self which should lead to a more complete self-revelation.

Any photographic approach which represents a response to a question such as "Who are you?" and "What does the good life mean to you?" invariably is asking the individual to "tell me more about yourself." Auto-photography permits others to view the world from the view of the observed persons. It is the view of "Me and my world" from the inside, as the "Me" views the world. In the process, the psychological niche of the observer is observed, but it is revealed nonverbally and in perpetuity. Thus photo-albums are a sort of photographic autobiography (see Akeret, 1973). One of the difficulties of interpreting photo-albums, however, is that we do not know what question is being asked or what question the photographer is asking him/herself. But it can be assumed that some event or experience of some significance is being frozen as it is happening in a natural setting.

A more systematic approach to observations of the view of an event from the inside, or the actor's view, is now possible by simply asking the actor to take a set of photographs during the course of a particular experience or event. This experience or event may be difficult for anyone but the experiencer to observe, or it may even be unethical for an observer to be present (such as the last three days of a marriage). Nevertheless the cases presented here offer a rare observation opportunity for an auto-photographic vignette. In the process, phenomena are explored and observed as they actually occur and as they are perceived by the perceiver. This vernacular approach to viewing events grew out of a study in which the photograph presented in Figure 6.1 emerged.

The photograph in Figure 6.1 was taken by a naive photographer who was asked to take a set of 12 photographs that describe "What the University of Florida campus means to you." In itself, the photograph certainly does not qualify as a work of art or as a subject of social science inquiry. It is only when the characteristics of the naive photographer become known that the photograph becomes both a work of art and science. The meaning of the photograph begins to emerge when it is learned that the photographer (responding to a specific question) is a college student who as a result of a diving accident a few years earlier is paralyzed and permanently confined to a wheelchair. Suddenly the viewer glimpses and even momentarily experiences the social field of the physically handicapped person. We are

Figure 6.1. The view from the wheelchair.

126

experiencing a social encounter between a man in a wheel chair and a collection of people.

It is unlikely that either the subjects in the photograph or the photographer were aware of the social transaction. The camera has recorded without blinking or reservation the silent communications between the handicapped person and the people surrounding him. There frozen before us is an existential scene of the strained efforts of the crowd of people to avoid eye contact with the handicapped photographer.

Perhaps they may not wish to betray a sense of sympathy. Or they may be responding to a distant parental admonition not to stare at someone who is handicapped. Thus, the handicapped person rarely establishes eye contact, or only sees averted eyes.

Through the eyes of the handicapped person we experience avoidance. We see bodies without eyes. We do not see a group but a wall of people (from wheelchair height, people are tall). We are viewing civil inattention.

The view from the wheel-chair was only one of the photographs taken by five wheelchair students who participated in a study comparing their views of the University of Florida campus with the views of a control group which consisted of 15 students from the same university (Ziller & Smith, 1977). The five wheelchair students were the total population of wheelchair students attending the university. They participated voluntarily and without any inducements. The 15 other students were volunteers from one dormitory at the same university. All were undergraduate students. The photographs were coded for "eye contact." The two coders were in complete agreement.

Only one photograph taken by a person in a wheelchair showed eye contact. On the other hand, 7 of 18 sets of photographs taken by subjects in the comparison group showed at least one photograph indicating eye contact between the photographer and persons in the photographic field. There were no observable differences between the two groups concerning the number of photographs involving people.

Again, this photograph dramatizes the effects of self-event interaction. We glimpse the actor's world as he/she views it at crucial points of person-social situation encounter. Indeed, phenomenologists propose that these encounters define meaning (Kockelmans, 1966, p. 63); that is, the impact of an encounter on the self. The impact here, I submit, is self-isolation, separation from others, all others. It is proposed that conditions of intense social encounters evoke some of the most profound facets of the self, facets which are most certainly unseen in most approaches to the study of the self.

It now behooves us to search for other social encounters which might be observed using the auto-photographic approach. It is anticipated that each encounter may elicit a new facet of the self in somewhat the same way as the impossible encounters between persons and events with no-win outcomes studied by Weiss (1975) led to the concept of "learned helplessness."

Release from Prison

In an effort to explore some particular high-impact encounter in order to discover particularly significant facets of the self as they are revealed in self-event interactions, the auto-photography task was presented to a person upon being released from prison. Again, it is assumed that intense encounters in interaction with the self bring the theory of the self into bold relief the better to be observed through the auto-photographic approach.

Procedure

It was learned that an acquaintance was to be released permanently from prison somewhat unexpectedly in order for him to attend to his father, who was in a hospital under intensive care. The subject was 25 years of age and had spent the previous 30 months in prison.

The person was contacted by the investigator about possible participation in the project. Upon his assent and prior to his release, the person was sent a self-focusing 35-mm camera with a built-in flash loaded with 24-exposure film. The person was asked "to take (or have taken) up to 24 photographs in the first three days following your release, beginning from the time of leaving the prison grounds. The photographs can of anything so long as they show what you are experiencing at the time over the three day period. We are not interested in your photographic ability, but only your views of the three day experience."

When the photographs were developed they were discussed with the subject using a photo-stimulated interview. The entire set of photographs was presented on a table before the subject in the sequence in which they were taken. The subject was asked to described what the photographs depicted and what his reactions were at the time the photographs were taken (see Figure 6.2).

In sequence, the photographs show his female friend in the car waiting to take him to his family home, a photograph of himself, of his mother waiting on the steps of their home, of his father in intensive care, of his sister's children, his guitar, his sister's dog behind a wire fence, and then a series of photos of his female friend while they are visiting a park.

The photographs show an orientation toward people, toward family, toward close relationships. These may be interpreted as the subject's recognition and appreciation of a strong support system, including family and female friend, or identification with significant others. The returnee shows himself as enveloped by significant others, in contrast, perhaps, to his previous isolation from significant others. Surely the sequence shows the social self, or the new psychological niche to which he has escaped.

There is also a certain simplicity about the photographs. The subject may be content at this point in his encounter

Figure 6.2. My first three days following release from prison.

with the real world to describe his psychological niche in terms of the family and friends as they were before his unexpected departure. This may represent his way of creating continuity following a violent disruption in life course. The photographs depict security in this very social niche. Perhaps, too, the photographs emphasize the immediate. Time is arrested, for now.

Perhaps, too, what is not shown is at least as significant as what is shown. Photographs of the community do not exist. There are no photographs of persons outside the family, people from the community. There are no aesthetic orientations. The psychological niche is relatively closed. Connections between the self and the community at large will take a little longer. For now, the family is enough.

The auto-photographic approach contrasts to the approach of the professional photographer, who might be expected to take many sets of photographs of the returnee over three days in order to record the reentry experience. In the auto-photograph approach, the actor selects those images which are of greatest significance from his/her point of view. Thus, through the nature of the known experience, the question posed, and the actor's orientations, the meaning of the photographs develops. The meaning emerges initially because the photographs are responses to a particular event (here, release from prison). Meaning is further clarified because the actor is asked to select the most significant images, simply by virtue of the number of film exposures. Finally, the orientations of the actor are recorded by the directed and focused camera. As a result of these three steps, the sets of photographs represent meaningful images depicting the actor's orientation in response to given life conditions. The images are the meaning of the experience for the actor. We are witnessing a photo-narrative of a dramatic experience, the son's return. But it is the son's view.

Interpretation

It is not enough to glance at the images and extract a meaningful concept. Even the concept of close relationship orientations does violence to the meaning of the set of photographs. The meaning of the auto-photographic narrative must emerge after vicarious immersion into the photo-experience. Only then will the meaning along with its emotional overtones evolve. The transfer of the experience from the actor to the observer is facilitated by realizing, remembering, and reminding ourselves as observers that it is the view of the viewer that we are viewing and experiencing.

Curiously, this requires an entirely different mind-set than viewing the work of a photographer who is often a mediator in the communication process. In auto-photography we have eliminated the middle person in the communication network. We are observing directly. As a result, we are observing a different reality. The images have a meaning which is in a different domain than what we are accustomed. Few of us have even seen a set of photographs taken by a subject in response to a question or to record an experience.

Susan Sontag (1977) has noted that for the Western civilization with its ubiquitous image communication, reality is the image. It is not real until it is photographed. It is proposed here that we cannot understand the auto-photographic narrative, or perhaps more accurately a vignette, unless the image is viewed as the actor views it.

In the next section, the search continues for significant aspects of the self as they are revealed in social encounters. One of the most significant social encounters surely must be that which involves a critical juncture in man-woman relations. It is assumed here that critical facets of the self may be revealed under these special conditions. The emergent critical concept is attachment.

Man-Woman Relationships

A theory of the self would be most incomplete if it did not include facets derived from encounters with intimate others. One such component might be the social self, but this hardly represents the quiddity of man-woman relation pertaining to the self. Self-concepts such as identification with intimate other or perception of self-other attachment (Bowlby, 1969) are perhaps more valid facets of the self in terms of their derivation from man-woman experiences. The search for such key concepts was conducted in the following three case studies, which describe the man-woman encounters of marriage, divorce, and transition to marriage. As already indicated, the central self-other concept is attachment.

In describing primary groups, Cooley (1909) stressed the component of intimacy among the members, but he seemed to assume that the concept—intimacy—was self-explanatory. Others have used related concepts, such as nexification (Laing, 1971), loyalty, commitment (Ziller, 1977), involvement, responsibility, meaning, and in-group/out-group boundaries. It is proposed here that a common element among these concepts is attachment. Attachment evolves in long-term groups when the self-concept of the individual becomes inextricably involved with the concept of another member of the group and the group as a unit (Ziller, 1977).

The study of attachment (Cohen, 1974) is concerned with a specific relationship—that between a person and his/her most intimate companion. It is usually proposed that the object of attachment serves a special psychological function for which others cannot substitute and that he/she elicits affective and social responses that differ from those elicited by others. The special relationship between mother and child or man and woman are two of the most poignant examples. Studies of depression following separation from those who are "special" illustrate the power of the relationship (Bowlby, 1969; Weiss, 1975).

Most studies of attachment, however, fail to operationalize adequately the feature of "specificity" or specialness. Moreover, the problem of operationalizing specificity becomes more complex when studying attachment among adults because of their complex cognitive processes. A clue has been suggested by Fairbain (1952), however. He observed in a clinical setting that an internal representation of the attachment figure becomes intertwined with the self. In these terms, if the self together with the other constitute the self-concept, separation from the "special" other person leads to a threat to the self-concept and also to associated outcomes, such as depression. Again we have recourse to Cooley's definition of primary groups in which he proposed that "the very self" is involved in primary group relations.

It is now proposed that the attachment and separation experience may be understood uniquely through utilization of the photographic self-concept of the experiencer.

Procedure

In the course of administering the "Who are you?" photographic task to a wide range of subjects and following this task with a photo-assisted interview, three cases involving marriage encounters were noted which were particularly intense. The first two cases concerned women both of whom had been married for 10 years, but the third case involved a set of photographs taken during therapy following divorce (see Figures 2.2 and 2.3).

Results

The first set of photographs (see Figure 2.4) describes a woman who has been married for 10 years, has two young children, lives in an upper-middle class neighborhood, and attends some classes at the local university.

The task was approached meticulously, and the photographs were arranged systematically in order of personal significance: the self first; next the husband and self; husband, self, and children; etc. The last photograph shows the subject studying alone. The self is first and last, but the remainder of the photographs are predominantly associated with husband, children, and home. The self is framed by significant others and also frames significant others. Signs of intimacy and attachment are noted in the large percentage of the photographs showing body contact among the family members. The most prominent signs may be that of structure and order, almost a plan. Little is left to chance. The major arrow of orientation is vertical: the trees, people standing, the trees by the building entrance. Everything is upright.

There is a direct simplicity about this set of photographs. The boundaries of the family are clearly defined. There are no other people and very few things (material orientation). The family is perceived as complete and exclusive. The self and significant others are mutually contained within the depicted psychological niche. The naive photographer is attached.

Separation

The second set of photographs (see Figure 2.3) was presented by a recently divorced woman who had been married for 10 years and whose husband had initiated the separation. No children were involved. The woman was under conditions of counseling. She too attended the same university.

The signs of the set of photographs include diffusion, pieces of times past (almost antique), of multiple directions and unclear paths with a few distant unknown people and offspring which are not one's own. There is a singular lack of activity and people. The mood is that of suspended animation between the beginning haze of the past and the future depicted as an uncharted infinity (see the first three photographs). The self is connected to the significant other only in time past, but even then the traces are to places and things, not directly to the other. The set of photographs represents the residual of past attachment and the uncertainty of the self in the present separation. The earlier, psychological niche appears to be fading, while the new psychological niche is yet to be developed. I submit that we are viewing alienation.

The last two sets of photographs (see Figures 6.3 and 6.4) are the self-representations of a woman about four years younger than the two preceding subjects. She was about to graduate from the same local university. She had been dating the same person for two years. One set of photographs was taken when there were serious doubts about their future together. The second set was taken four weeks later following their decision to marry. They were married six weeks later. The subject had taken the final set of photographs as part of a class exercise (the same class as the first subject), but later voluntarily reported that the set of photographs was not representative and asked to take a second set.

The signs or meanings of the first set of photographs taken under conditions of transition show no friends, do not include the self or the long-time friend, or any very significant possessions such as cat, camper, or plants. In fact, few things seem to be the direct target of the photographer. The photographer seems to lack attention or concentration. It is noted that there is considerable similarity to the preceding photographs of alienation, or perhaps less evaluatively, of the self in transition.

The signs of the second set show much greater activity with the future spouse and involve elements of her life which are significant: the cat, camper, plants, and bicycle. Intimacy and attachment as coded from photos that involve body contact are shown only in the second set of photographs. The last photograph symbolizes their plan to search the United States for a most suitable place to settle, a direction, and a future. The self-concept reflects the change from doubt to direction through identification with the significant other.

Summary

This semiotic analysis of the sets of photographs provides some clues for increased understanding of some aspects of

Figure 6.3. The photographic self-concept of a woman in transition.

Figure 6.4. The photographic self-concept of a woman about to be married.

the lives of women through perceiving the perceiver and searching for signs phenomenologically. The signs of attachment are a bonding and bracketing of the self and significant other: boundaries, activity, direction, structure, a time orientation to the present and future, a surcease in the search for another in finding the other (no friends or strangers are included in the photos), perhaps even an inward orientation and exclusion of all others because of a sense of completeness.

In contrast, the signs of separation are the lack of self and others as points of reference, and boundaries or framing devices; a lack of activity; concentration on the past and avoidance of the future; and a sense of the undirected, unfocused, and incomplete. Connections between the self and others are indistinct, and new connections are beyond consideration. The future is shown as an uncharted infinity.

The concepts of attachment, separation, and transition are presented visually, and by dwelling upon the visual arrays, the signs and their meaning emerge, but not rapidly. The increased understanding of attachment separation and transition emerges only when the set of photographs is experienced, and when the viewer identifies with the photographer. Only then can the perceiver be perceived and understanding begin. Indeed, an improved understanding of persons under conditions of attachment and separation can be developed through their photographic self-concepts but not without repeated familiarization with the photographs over time and a readiness to search for personal understanding simultaneously.

Overview

The three case studies involving photo-communication were conducted in an effort to explore the orientations and associated self-concepts of the naive photographer. It was assumed that the observation from the inside out of intense social encounters affords a unique opportunity to discover critical self-other concepts. The events selected for analysis included a social encounter of a man in a wheelchair with a collection of people in a public place; three days in the life of a person, beginning with his release from prison; and finally marriage, divorce, and transition to marriage. The crucial self-other concepts that were revealed included social separation, social support, and attachment.

In these case studies, the investigator utilized a reflexive approach wherein the subject discussed the meaning of the photographs with the investigator, using a photo-assisted interview. Nevertheless, the interpretation of the photographs is not without difficulty, although this may be advantageous in that understanding is seen as a continuous process. Moreover, the case studies were exploratory and designed to discover significant self-other concepts.

I propose that the primary obstacle to the interpretation of these photographs of the self is the imposition of inappropriate image interpretation rules on these self-photographs, rules derived from television and movie experiences as well as photo-album experiences. The auto-photography task may appear similar because the product is an image, but that is misleading. Auto-photography involves a naive photographer responding to a specific question. It is well to be reminded continuously that a third party, a professional photographer, is not involved. One concrete step toward better understanding of the nature of photographing the self is actually to perform the ''Who am I?'' task with a camera. Unfortunately, however, the experience is already vitiated by the very fact that the reader is no longer naive, a fundamental requirement of the task.

CHAPTER
7

Conclusion

It is proposed here that in the process of presenting photographs of the self the psychological niche of the naive photographer is revealed. The psychological niche is described in a triadic model of Environment-Self-Behavior Theory, where the self is the major control mechanism which maintains unity among the three components. The theory of the self is an omnibus schema representing a system of personal postulates, principles, and rules which organizes and regulates behavior within a given environment.

This framework along with the accompanying inside-out photo-observation approach introduces a new view of the self-concept. Here the self-concept is not an isolated concept but part of an Environment-Self-Behavior system in which the underlying motivation is control. The self as the nucleus component is the central control mechanism. The self is agenetic. The self theory is associated with a repertoire of behaviors consistent with the self theory, and it leads to orientations of the environment meaningful to the self. The resulting system is the psychological niche which defines the region of control. It must be underscored that the environment is not only a significant component of the system but retains its significance in the research emanating from the theory because of the unique characteristics of the apparatus used—the camera. Like no other personality instrument, the camera (along with the questions) envelops the subject in the environment.

The interactive construct between the self and the environment is orientations. Orientations are behaviors associated with self definition which indicate increased motivation to respond to certain signs in the environment. Selected objects, persons, and symbols in the environment serve to reaffirm the self, thereby providing an environment which is not alien.

The nature of orientations are somewhat idiosyncratic, but owing to the commonality of environment and human experience, some universal orientations are posited, such as self, social, and aesthetic. In some sense, then, orientations and personal constructs are similar.

Indeed this similarity led to an expanded definition of the self concept to include a wide range of orientations and personal constructs revealed by asking the persons to respond with photographs to questions such as the meaning of "woman," "war," and "the good life," which evoked self-orientation associations which were barred in previous research, leading to a restricted theory of the self. Studies of the differential meaning of critical concepts must be extended, along with case studies of self-event interaction, in an effort to extend the theory of the self and the theory of the psychological niche.

By emphasizing the omnibus schema of the self, the cognitive concept of orientations, and the processing of information within the natural environment, the theory of the self with its cognitive base places the approach within the new cognitive emphasis in social psychology. More importantly, however, the psychological niche theory involving the motivation to control may bracket a host of research findings from all the social sciences.

Future Research

The theory and accompanying photographic observation approach is an invitation to creativity. The research program should be extended to the study of the meaning of other crucial or ineffable concepts. For example, older and younger persons' orientations with regard to "their community" may be compared. Differences in the meaning of "What is beauty?" should be explored.

The approach is particularly useful in cross-cultural studies, as has been demonstrated here, but these studies need to be extended to other countries and other special groups as well, to help explicate differences in the self and differences in other crucial concepts such as "the good life" or "me and my world." By using this approach with a sample of persons from a variety of nations and cultures, similarities and differences in orientations and self theories among people of the earth may be illustrated.

Furthermore, the theory of orientations now can be tested under field conditions. For example, it is hypothesized that high-frequency orienting increases the importance of these orientations. High-frequency orienting can be accomplished by asking the subject to take a large number of photographs of a particular kind, such as of a particular person or object in comparison with a control group which is asked to take on an equally large number of photographs about a general theme. It is proposed that orientation frequency per se is associated with attitude change.

Another research strategy is to emphasize certain facets of the self that emerge, particularly in using the Environment-Self-Behavior theory and the photographic observation approach. For example, orientation toward objects such as cars, home, equipment, clothes, and jewelry may be described as material orientation. Cross-cultural differences in material orientations are easily proposed, but other behaviors, including purchasing behavior or reduced emphasis on interpersonal relations by materially oriented persons, are hypothesized.

Unsolved Puzzles

Two major problems obtain. The first involves the large number of orientations which results as a function of self-environment interaction. The second, of course, concerns the interpretation of images.

The problem of the number of orientations is a result of the idiosyncratic nature of the person-situation interaction. Individual experiences as represented in the self-concept vary greatly, as do the individual environments, resulting in a vast array of potential orientations. Science abhors idiosyncracies. A search is indicated for a rationale to group the orientations.

Personal construct theory shares the problem of a plethora of potential constructs but views this characteristic as a virtue in that the framework is responsive to individual differences. Thus, the theory of the psychological niche could be supported by the same virtue argument. The latter, however, is indeed a self theory which assumes, at least, a personal systematization of orientations. Thus, it was proposed that there exists a hierarchy of orientations for shy persons, for example, and presumably this hierarchy evolves from some underlying personal framework.

This points to the logical source of a classification system for orientation--the underlying self theory. The orientations stem from self-environment interaction. The first approximation to a category system for orientations is most easily derived from an analysis of the environment. Indeed, using a simple classification of self, social, and environmental orientations, the questions posed to the naive photographer were selected because the orientations that could be developed would lead to a more complete theory of the self. For example, value orientations and gender orientations emerged as core facets of the self when diverse questions of meaning were posed. It remains to present these questions and resulting orientations more systematically.

The final puzzle is the interpretation of the images. As I have described, the difficulty is somewhat reduced because the photographs here are in response to a question, thereby directing the attention of the interpreter to some degree. In addition, a number of photographs are usually submitted in response to the bracketing question, which introduces the possibility of redundancy which may help to decode the message in images. Finally, earlier work concerning the interpretation of dreams, as well as the research involving the "Who are you?" task provide some bases for interpretation.

Of course, there is always the respondent's own interpretations of their photographs through "photo-assisted interviews." This approach proved indispensable in some of the studies, particularly the case studies. But if the naive photographer is informed of the interview before taking the photographs, the photo-communication task is changed markedly because the respondent need not be as assiduous in selecting photos which best communicate the intended message. In addition, images without words may counterintuitively provide the respondent a means to be more self-disclosing.

In fact, the ability to interpret a photograph in a wide variety of ways provides a defensive position for the communicator, who may feel more free to express his/her feelings more candidly, if you will. Thus, the difficulty of interpretation is not entirely disadvantageous.

Certainly, the optimum approach is to follow the example of research on nonverbal communication (see Ekman, 1973, for example) and to validate the various images experimentally as indeed was the case here in the study of shyness and social orientations. These validity studies must be extended with regard to other categories, especially aesthetics, social orientation, and values, including material orientation.

Again, however, this is not to suggest that an image dictionary be developed. Given the variety of orientations, new interpretations will always be required, as was exemplified in the study of American versus Polish values, where private versus institutional values were posited. Indeed, some of the most significant outcomes of this research program arose heuristically. The studies of the meaning of war and peace, and the Polish-American values studies are probably the best examples. The greatest advantage of photo-communication is, in fact, as an aid in the discovery process. It is no accident that observation approaches in general possess this quality.

A Final Word

Research may be evaluated in a wide variety of ways, including its contribution to theory, its applicability, its adherence to scientific principles, or even in terms of being "mainstream psychology." The criterion I have used in evaluating my research efforts is the degree of my personal excitement generated by the search. This research has been exhilarating! No small part of the satisfaction was derived from developing a theory and approach which I believe help us understand others from their point of view, the sine qua non for human understanding.

References

Akeret, R. V. (1973). *Photoanalysis*. New York: Peter H. Wyden.

Allen, V. L., & Wilder, D. A. (1975). Categorization, belief similarity, and group discrimination. *Journal of Personality and Social Psychology, 32,* 971-977.

Alper, T. G. (1964). Ego-orientation in learning and retention. *American Journal of Psychology, 59,* 236-248.

Alvik, T. (1968). The development of youth on conflict, war, and peace among school children (a Norwegian case study). *Journal of Peace Research, 3,* 171-195.

Amerikaner, M., Schauble, P., & Ziller, R. C. (1980). Images: The use of photographs in counseling. *Personnel and Guidance Journal, 59,* 68-73.

Ames, L. B. (1940). The constancy of psychomotor tempo in individual infants. *Journal of Genetic Psychology, 57,* 445-450.

Bailyn, L. (1970). Career and family orientation of husbands and wives in relation to marital happiness. *Human Relations, 23,* 97-113.

Bandura, A. (1977). *Social learning theory*. Englewood Cliffs, NJ: Prentice-Hall.

Bandura, A. (1987). The self and the mechanisms of agency. In J. Suls (Ed.), *Psychological perspectives on the self*. Hillsdale, NJ: Erlbaum.

Bargh, J. A. (1982). Attention and automaticity in processing of self-relevant information. *Journal of Personality and Social Psychology, 43,* 425-436.

Barker, R. G., & Wright, H. F. (1955). *Midwest and its children*. Evanston, IL: Row, Peterson.

Barthes, R. (1985). Rhetoric of the image. In R. E. Innis (Ed.), *Semiotics: An introductory anthology*. Bloomington: Indiana University Press.

Bateson, G., & Mead, M. (1942). *Balinese character: A photographic analysis*. New York: New York Academy of Sciences Special Publication.

Becker, H. S. (1981). *Exploring society photographically*. Evanston, IL: Mary and Leigh Block Gallery.

Berkowitz, L. (1988). *Advances in experimental social psychology*, (Vol. 21). New York: Academic Press.

Biddle, B. J., & Thomas, E. J. (Eds.). (1966). *Role theory: Concepts and research*. New York: John Wiley.

Blyton, P. (1987). The image of work: Documentary photography and the production of "reality." *International Social Science Journal, 39,* 15-424.

Bowlby, J. (1969). *Attachment and loss* (Vol. 1) *Attachment*. London: Hogarth.

Brehmen, B. (1976). Social judgment theory and analysis of interpersonal conflict. *Psychological Bulletin, 83,* 985- 1003.

Broverman, I. K., Vogel, S. R., Broverman, D. M., Clarkson, F. E., & Rosenkrantz, P. S. (1972). Sex-role stereotypes: A current appraisal. *Journal of Social Issues, 28,* 59-78.

Bugental, J. F. T., & Zelen, S. L. (1950). Investigations into the self-concept. *Journal of Personality, 18,* 483-498.

Cairnes, E. (1980). "Non-verbal indicators of the self-concept of Catholic and Protestant children in Northern Ireland" (unpublished paper, University of Ulster: Northern Ireland).

Campbell, C. (1983). Taking a picture. *Sociology and Photography International, 1,* 8-13.

Carver, C. S., & Scheirer, M. F. (1981). *Attention and self-regulation: A control theory approach to human behavior*. New York: Springer.

Cattell, R. B. (1973). *Personality and mood by questionnaire*. San Francisco: Josey-Bass.

Chalfen, R. (1974). *Photoanalysis studies in the anthropology of visual communication,* 5, 57-59.

Cohen, L. J. (1974). The operational definition of human attachment. *Psychological Bulletin, 84,* 207-217.

Collier, J., Jr. (1975). *Visual anthropology: Photography as a research method.* New York: Holt, Rinehart, & Winston.

Collier, J., & Collier, M. (1986). *Visual anthropology: Photography as a research method.* Albuquerque: University of New Mexico Press.

Collins, G. M., & Shaffer, H. R. (1975). Synchronization of visual attention in mother-infant pairs. *Journal of Childhood Psychology and Psychiatry, 16,* 315-320.

Combs, J., & Ziller, R. C. (1977). The photographic self-concept of counselees. *Journal of Counseling Psychology, 24,* 452- 455.

Cooley, C. H. (1909). *Social organization.* New York: Charles Scribner.

Cooper, P. (1965). The development of the concept of war. *Journal of Peace Research,* 1, 1-17.

Creelman, M. B. (1966). *The experimental investigation of meaning.* New York: Springer.

Crozier, W. R. (1979). Shyness as a dimension of personality. *British Journal of Social and Clinical Psychology, 18,* 121-128.

Damico, S. B. (1985). The two worlds of school: Differences in the photographs of Black and White adolescents. *The Urban Review, 17,* 210-222.

Deese, J. (1965). *The structure of associations in language and thought.* Baltimore, MD: Johns Hopkins University Press.

Dencker, K. (1939). Ethical relativity of an inquiry into the psychology of ethics. *Minch, 48,* 39-57.

Deutch, M. (1960). The effect of motivational orientations on trust and suspicion. *Human Relations, 13,* 111-139.

Dickie, G. (1964). All aesthetic attitude theories fail: The myth of the aesthetic attitude. *American Philosophical Quarterly, 1,* 56-66.

Diener, E., Larsen, R. J., & Emmons, R. A. (1984). Person x situation interactions: Choice of situations and congruence response models. *Journal of Personality and Social Psychology, 47,* 580-592.

Dinklage, R. L., & Ziller, R. C. (1989). Explicating cognitive conflict through photo-communication: The meaning of war and peace in Germany and the United States. *Journal of Conflict Resolution, 32,* 1-19.

Dittman, A. T. (1962). The relationship between body movements and mood in interviews. *Journal of Consulting Psychology, 26,* 480-491.

Dittman, A. T. (1972). Speech and body motion. In A. Seigman & B. Pope (Eds.), *Studies in dyadic communication.* Elmsford, NY: Pergamon Press.

Dittman, A. T., Parloff, M. B., & Boomer, D. S. (1965). Facial and bodily expression: A study of receptivity of emotional cues. *Psychiatry, 28,* 239-244.

Douglas, J. D. (1976). *Investigative social research.* Beverly Hills, CA: Sage.

Duval, S., & Wicklund, R. A. (1972). *A theory of objective self-awareness.* New York: Academic Press.

Ekman, P. (Ed.). (1973). *Darwin and facial expression: A century of research in review.* New York: Academic Press.

Ekman P., & Friesen, W. (1974). Detecting deception from the body or face. *Journal of Personality and Social Psychology, 29,* 288-289.

Epstein, S. (1973). The self-concept revisited: Or a theory of a theory. *American Psychologist, 19,* 404-416.

Estes, S. G. (1938). Judging personality from expressive behavior. *Journal of Abnormal and Social Psychology, 33,* 212-236.

Fairbain, W. R. D. (1952). *Psychoanalytic studies of personality.* Boston: Routledge & Kegan.

Freedman, N., & Hoffman, S. P. (1967). Kinetic behavior in altered clinical states: An approach to objective analysis of motor behavior during clinical interviews. *Perceptual and Motor Skills, 24,* 527-539.

Freud, S. (1924). *Collected papers.* London: Hogarth.

Furnham, A., & Argyle, M. (1981). *The psychology of social situations.* Oxford: Pergamon Press.

Gardner, R. (1963). *Dead birds.* Film distributed by Phoenix.

Gergen, K. J. (1973). Social psychology as history. *Journal of Personality and Social Psychology, 26,* 309-320.

Gergen, K. J., & Gergen, N. M. (1988). The self as known: Narrative and self as relationships. In L. Berkowitz (Ed.), *Advances in experimental social psychology* (Vol. 21) (pp. 17-56). New York: Academic Press.

Gesell, A. L. (1945). Cinemanalysis: A method of behavior study. *Journal of General Psychology, 47,* 3.

Gesell, A. L., & Ames, L. B. (1937). Early evidence of individuality in the human infant. *Scientific Monthly, 45,* 217-225.

Gibbons, F. X., & Wicklund, R. A. (1987). Self-focused attention and helping behavior. *Journal of Personality and Social Psychology, 43,* 462-474.

Gibson, J. J. (1979). *The ecological approach to visual perception.* Boston: Houghton Mifflin.

Gillespie-Waltemade, N. (1984). Power, politics, and photography: Issues in teaching visual sociology. *Humanity and Society, 8,* 385-392.

Gilligan, R. C. (1982). *In a different voice: Psychological theory and women's development.* Cambridge, MA: Harvard University Press.

Goffman, E. (1974). *Frame analysis.* New York: Harper & Row.

Gordon, C., & Gergen, K. J. (Eds.). (1968). *The self in social interaction.* New York: John Wiley.

Gross, L. (1980). Sol Worth and the study of visual communication. *Visual Communication, 6,* 2-19.

Haavedsrud, M. (1970). Views on war and peace among students in West Berlin public schools. *Journal of Peace Research, 2,* 99-120.

Hall, C. S., & Van DeCastle, R. V. (1966). *The content analysis of dreams.* Englewood Cliffs, NJ: Prentice-Hall.

Hastie, R. (1983). Social inference. In *Annual Review of Psychology* (Vol. 34). Palo Alto, CA: Annual Reviews.

Hays, W. L. (1973). *Statistics for the social sciences.* New York: Holt, Rinehart, & Winston.

Heider, K. G. (1976). *Ethnographic film.* Austin: University of Texas Press.

Heisenberg, N. (1958). *The physicist's conception of nature.* London: Hutchinson.

Hine, L. W. (1932). *Men at work.* New York: Macmillan.

Hunt, W. A. (1936). Studies of the startle pattern: II, Bodily pattern. *Journal of Psychology, 2,* 207-213.

Ickes, W., Robertson, E., Tooke, W., & Teng, G. (1986). Naturalistic social cognition: Methology, assessment, and validation. *Journal of Personality and Social Psychology, 50,* 66-82.

Jacob, P. E. (1957). *Changing values in college: An exploratory study of the impact of college teaching.* New York: Harper.

James, W. (1890). *Principles of psychology.* New York: Holt, Rinehart, & Winston.

Jeffrey, W. E. (1968). The orienting reflex and attention in cognitive development. *Psychological Review, 75,* 323-334.

Jourard, S. M. (1964). *The transparent self.* New York: Van Nostrand.

Kahn, P. (1966). Time orientation and perceptual and cognitive organization. *Perceptual and Motor Skills, 23,* 1059-1066.

Kahneman, D., & Tversky, A. (1972). Subjective probability: A judgment of representationes. *Cognition Psychology, 3,* 430-454.

Katz, J. (1968). *No time for youth.* San Francisco: Jossey-Bass.

Kelly, G. A. (1955). *The psychology of personal constructs.* New York: Norton.

Kendon, A. (1979). Some theoretical and methodological aspects of the use of film in the study of social interactions. In G. P. Ginsburg (Ed.), *Emerging strategies in social psychological research* (pp. 67-91). New York: John Wiley.

Kennedy, J. M. (1974). *The psychology of picture perception.* San Francisco: Jossey-Bass.

Kluckhohn, C. (1951). Values and value orientations in the theory of action. In T. Parson & Shils (Eds.), *Toward a general theory of action* (pp. 388-433). Cambridge, MA: Harvard University Press.

Kockelmans, J. (1966). *Phenomenology and physical science.* Pittsburgh: Duquesne University Press.

Koffka, K. (1935). *Gestalt psychology.* New York: Harcourt, Brace.

Kraus, D. A., & Fryrear, J. L. (Eds.). (1983). *Phototherapy in mental health.* Springfield, IL: Charles C Thomas.

Krippendorff, K. (1980). *Content analysis: An introduction to its methodology.* Beverly Hills, CA: Sage.

Kuhn, M. H., & McPartland, T. S. (1954). An empirical investigation of self-attitudes. *American Sociological Review, 19,* 68-76.

Kupperman, H. S. (1967). The endocrine status of the transsexual patient. *Transactions of the New York Academy of Science, 29,* 434-439.

Laing, R. D. (1971). *The politics of the family and other essays.* New York: Pantheon.

Laing, R. D., & Esterson, A. (1964). *Sanity, madness and the family: Families of schizophrenics.* London: Tavistock.

Landis, C. (1924). Studies of emotional reactions: II, General behavior and facial expression. *Journal of Comparative Psychology, 4,* 447-509.

Leary, M. R., & Schlenker, B. R. (1981). The social psychology of shyness: A self-presentational model. In J. J. Tedeschi (Ed.), *Impression management theory and social psychological research* (pp. 335-357). New York: Academic Press.

Levelt, W. J. M. (1968). *On binocular rivalry.* The Hague: Houton.

Levy, L. H. (1963). *Psychological interpretation.* New York: Holt, Rinehart, & Winston.

Lewis, M. E., & Butler, R. N. (1974). Life review therapy. *Geriatrics,* November, 165-173.

Lomax, A. (1968). *Folksong style and culture.* Washington, DC: American Association for the Advancement of Science, Publication No. 88.

Lyddon, W. J. (1988). Information-processing and constructivist models of cognitive therapy: A philosophical divergence. *Journal of Mind and Behavior, 9,* 137-165.

Martindale, A. (1960). *The nature and types of sociological theory.* Boston: Houghton Mifflin.

McDonald, P. J., & Eilenfield, V. C. (1980). Physical attractiveness and the approach/avoidance of self-awareness. *Personality and Social Psychology Bulletin, 6,* 391-395.

McKinney, J. P. (1979). Photo counseling. *Children Today, 8,* 29.

Mead, G. H. (1934). *Mind, self, and society.* Chicago: University of Chicago Press.

Merton, R. D. (1949). Patterns of influence: A study of interpersonal influence and of communications, behavior in a social community. In P. F. Lazarsfeld & V. Stanton (Eds.), *Communications research, 1948-1949,* (102-141). New York: Harper.

Michaels, A. R. (1955). *Research films in biology, anthropology, psychology, and medicine.* New York: Academic Press.

Milgram, S. (1977). The image freezing machine. *Psychology Today, 108,* 50-54.

Mischel, W. (1977). On the future of personality measurement. *American Psychologist, 32,* 246-254.

Monson, T. C., Hesley, J. W., & Chernick, L. (1982). Specifying when personality can and cannot predict behavior: An alternative to abandoning the attempt to predict single-act criteria. *Journal of Personality and Social Psychology, 43,* 385-399.

Morris, C. (1946). *Signs, language and behavior.* New York: Prentice-Hall.

Mueller, W. J. (1973). *Avenues to understanding: The dynamics of therapeutic interaction.* New York: Appleton-Century-Crofts.

Murphy, G. (1947). *Personality.* New York: Harper and Brothers.

Neimeyer, R. A. (1987). An orientation to personal construct theory. In R. A. Neimeyer & G. J. Neimeyer (Eds.), *Personal construct theory casebook,* (1-31). New York: Springer.

Nielsen, G. (1964). *Studies in self-confrontation.* Copenhagen: Munksgaard.

O'Grady, K. E. (1982). Sex, physical attractiveness, and perceived risk for mental illness. *Journal of Personality and Social Psychology, 43,* 1064-1071.

Ortony, A., & Reynolds, R. E. (1978). Metaphor: Theoretical and empirical research. *Psychological Bulletin, 85,* 919-943.

Pavlov, I. P. (1927). *Conditioned reflexes.* Oxford: Clarendon Press.

Pelz, H. (1974). *The scope of understanding in sociology.* London: Routledge & Kegan.

Petrie, H. (1979). Metaphor and learning. In A. Ortony (Ed.), *Metaphor and thought* (pp. 438-461). Cambridge: Cambridge University Press.

Pribram, K. H. (1971). *Languages of the brain.* Englewood Cliffs, NJ: Prentice-Hall.

Reeves, J. W. (1958). *Body and mind in western thought.* Baltimore, MD: Penguin Books.

Reisman, D. (1958). The "Jacob Report." *American Sociological Review, 23,* 732-738.

Rescher, N. (1969). *Introduction to value theory.* Englewood Cliffs, NJ: Prentice-Hall.

Riis, J. A. (1971). *How the other half lives.* New York: Dover (originally published in 1890).

Ring, K. (1967). Experimental social psychology: Some sober questions about some frivolous values. *Journal of Experimental Social Psychology, 3,* 113-123.

Rogers, C. R. (1951). *Client centered therapy.* Boston: Houghton Mifflin.

Rokeach, M. (1973). *The nature of human values.* New York: Free Press.

Rorer, B. A., & Ziller, R. C. (1982). The iconic communication of values. *Journal of Cross-Cultural Psychology, 13*, 352-361.

Rosell, L. (1968). Children's views of war and peace. *Journal of Peace Research, 3*, 268-276.

Rosenthal, R. (1976). *Experimenter effects in behavioral research* (2nd ed.). New York: Halsted Press.

Rothbart, M., Dawes, R., & Park, B. (1984). Stereotyping and sampling biases in intergroup perception. In J. R. Eisen (Ed.), *Attitudinal judgment* (pp. 224-260). New York: Gringer.

Rubin, Z. (1973). *Liking and loving: An invitation to social psychology.* New York: Holt, Rinehart, & Winston.

Ruesch, J., & Kees, W. (1956). *Nonverbal communication: Notes on the visual perception of human relations.* Berkeley: University of California Press.

Sauun, K. G. (Ed.), (1983). *Jahrbuch der offentlichen Meinung.* Allensbach am Bodensee: Verlag fur Demostcopie, Zerlag, Munich.

Sebeok, T. A. (1978). *The sign and its masters.* Austin: University of Texas Press.

Selltiz, C., Christ, J. R., Havel, J., & Cook, S. W. (1963). *Attitudes and social relations of foreign students in the United States.* Minneapolis: University of Minnesota Press.

Smith, D. E., Potter, R. H., & Ziller, R. C. (1978). "Self-Other: A photographic approach" (unpublished paper, University of Florida).

Smith, M. B. (1969). *Social psychology and human values.* Chicago: Aldine.

Snyder, M. (1981). On the influences of individuals on situations. In N. Cantor & J. Kihlstrom (Eds.), *Personality, cognition, and social interaction* (pp. 309-329). Hillsdale, NJ: Erlbaum.

Sokolov, E. N. (1963). *Perception and the conditioned reflex.* New York: Macmillan.

Sontag, S. (1977). *On photography.* New York: Farrar, Strauss, & Giroux.

Stryker, S. (1980). *Symbolic interactionism.* Menlo Park, CA: Benjamin-Cummings.

Stryker, S., & Statham, A. (1985). Symbolic interaction and role theory. In G. Lindsbey & E. Aronson (Eds.), *Handbook of social psychology* (Vol. 1) (pp. 311-378). New York: Random House.

Svancarova, L., & Svancarova, J. (1967-1968). Expression of peace and war in children's drawing and verbalizations. Translation from Russian in *Children in Conflict.* ERIC, 1983, 44, Abstract No. 166321.

Sway W. C., & Rubin, J. Z. (1983). Measurement of interpersonal orientation. *Journal of Personality and Social Psychology, 44*, 208-219.

Szczepanski, J. (1970). *Polish society.* New York: Random House.

Tajfel, H. (1970). Experiments in intergroup discrimination. *Scientific American, 223*, 96-102.

Tajfel, H. (1978). *Differentiation between social groups: Studies in the social psychology of intergroup relations.* New York: Academic Press.

Thompson, J. (1940). Development of facial expression of emotion in blind and seeing children. *Archives of Psychology, 37*, 1-47.

Titchener, E. B. (1909). *Lectures on the experimental psychology of thought processes.* New York: Macmillan.

Trent, J. W., & Craise, J. L. (1967). Commitment and conformity in the American college. *Journal of Social Issues, 23*, 34-51.

Triandis, H. C., & Berry, J. W. (Eds.). (1980). *Handbook of cross-cultural psychology:*

Methodology. Boston: Allyn & Bacon.

Turner, J. C. (1981). The experimental social psychology of intergroup behavior. In J. C. Turner & H. Giles (Eds.), *Intergroup behavior*. Oxford: Basil Blackwell.

Wachtel, P. (1973). Psychodynamics, behavior theory, and the implacable experimenter: An inquiry into the consistency of personality. *Journal of Abnormal Psychology, 82*, 324-334.

Wagner, J. (1979). *Images of information*. Beverly Hills, CA: Sage.

Walster (Hatfield) E., Aronson, V., Abrahams, D., & Rottman, L. (1966). Importance of physical attractiveness in dating behavior. *Journal of Personality and Social Psychology, 4*, 508-516.

Warren, H. C. (1916). Mental association from Plato to Hume. *Psychological Review, 23*, 208-230.

Weal, E. (1980). Photo psychology. *Innovations, 6*, 13-15.

Weick, K. E. (1985). Systematic observational methods. In G. Lindsey & E. Aronson (Eds.), *Handbook of social psychology* (Vol. 1) (pp. 567-634). New York: Random House.

Weiss, R. S. (1975). *Marital separation*. New York: Basic Books.

Wicklund, R. A. (1975). Objective self-awareness. In L. Berkowitz (Ed.), *Advances in experimental social psychology*, Vol. 8. New York: Academic Press.

Wilder, D. A. (1984). Prediction of belief homogeneity and similarity following social categorization. *British Journal of Social Psychology, 23*, 323-333.

Williams, R. (1979). Change and stability in values and value systems: A sociological perspective. In M. Rokeach (Ed.), *Understanding human values* (pp. 15-46). New York: Free Press.

Winget, C., & Kramer, M. (1979). *Dimensions of dreams*. Gainesville: University Presses of Florida.

Wolf, R. (1976). The Polaroid technique: Spontaneous dialogues from the unconscious. *Art Psychotherapy, 3*, 197-201.

Worth, S. (1964). Public administration and documentary film. *Journal of Municipal Association for Management and Administration, 1*, 19-25.

Worth, S., & Adair J. (1972). *Through Navajo eyes: An exploration in film communication and anthropology*. Bloomington: Indiana University Press.

Wundt, W. (1883). Uber psychologische Methoden. *Philosophische Studien, 1*, 11-38.

Ziller, R. C. (1973). *The social self*. New York: Pergamon.

Ziller, R. C. (1977). Group dialectics: The dynamics of groups over time. *Human Development, 20*, 293-308.

Ziller, R. C. (1988). Orientations: The cognitive link in person-situation interactions. *Journal of Social Behavior and Personality, 1*, 1-18.

Ziller, R. C., Martel, R. T., & Morrison, R. H. (1977). Social insulation, self-complexity, and social attraction: A theory chain. *Journal of Research in Personality, 11*, 398-415.

Ziller, R. C., & Smith, D. E. (1977). A phenomenological utilization of photographs. *Journal of Phenomenological Psychology, 7*, 172-185.

Ziller, R. C., & Lewis, D. (1981). Orientation: Self, social, and environmental percepts through auto-photography. *Personality and Social Psychology Bulletin, 7*, 338-343.

Ziller, R. C., & Rorer, B. A. (1985). Shyness-environment interaction: A view from the shy side through auto-photograph. *Journal of Personality, 53*, 626-639.

Ziller, R. C., & Okura, Y. (1986). The psychological niche of older Japanese and Americans through auto-photographs: Aging and the search for peace. *The International Journal of Aging and Human Development, 4*, 247-259.

Ziller, R. C., Vera, H., & Santoya, C. C. (1989). The psychological niche of children of poverty or affluence through auto-photography. *Children's Environments Quarterly, 6*, 186-196.

Ziller, R. C., Okura, Y., & Burns, A. (1989). "Perceptions of the United States among four nations through photo-communication" (unpublished paper, University of Florida).

Zimbardo, P. B. (1977). *Shyness.* Reading, MA: Addison-Wesley.

Author Index

Subject Index

About the Author

Robert C. Ziller is a Professor of Psychology at the University of Florida. He has written approximately 100 articles on the topics of individual-group conflict, group decision making, long-term groups, the self-concept, and photo-observation. An earlier book is *The Social Self* (1973). Currently he is studying universal orientation.